SHAKESPEARE'S PLAYS TODAY

'THE FOREST LOVERS'

Leon Quartermaine as Lysander, Athene Seyler as Hermia, Edith
Evans as Helena, Frank Vosper as Demetrius, in Basil Dean's
production of *A Midsummer Night's Dream* at Drury Lane, 1924.

SHAKESPEARE'S PLAYS TODAY

Some Customs and Conventions of the Stage

by

ARTHUR COLBY SPRAGUE

and

J. C. TREWIN

SIDGWICK & JACKSON
LONDON

First published 1970

Copyright © 1970 Authur Colby Sprague and J. C. Trewin

SBN 283.98091.5

Printed in Great Britain
by Spottiswoode, Ballantyne and Co. Ltd., London and Colchester
for Sidgwick and Jackson Limited
1 Tavistock Chambers, Bloomsbury Way
London, W.C.1

FOR W. AND P.

Contents

List of Plates		8
Preface		9
Introduction		11
I	STAGE BUSINESS	21
II	CUTTING THE TEXT	36
III	ADDITIONS TO THE TEXT	51
IV	SPEAKING THE LINES	66
V	SIGHTS AND SOUNDS	77
VI	THE PEOPLE OF THE PLAYS	92
VII	STAGES AND STAGING	107
Notes		124
Index of Persons		137
Index of Plays		144

List of Plates

To face page

Frontispiece 'THE FOREST LOVERS'   3

1.   'VILLIAN, BE SURE THOU PROVE MY LOVE A WHORE'   32

2.   THE PARTING OF HASTINGS AND JANE SHORE   33

3.   THE INDIAN BOY   48

4.   BARBARA JEFFORD AS ISABELLA   49

5.   A WINTRY WINDSOR   64

6.   A BAREFOOT AUDREY   65

7.   DON JOHN IN BLACK   80

8.   MALVOLIO AND THE REVELLERS   81

ACKNOWLEDGEMENTS

The plates are from the following sources:

A Midsummer Night's Dream (1924), from *The Bystander*, 7 January 1925, in Harvard Theatre Collection; *Othello* (1951), from a photograph by John Vickers; *Richard III* (1966) from a photograph supplied by Miss Mary Wallace; Charles Kean's *A Midsummer Night's Dream* (1856) from *The Illustrated London News*, 6 December 1856; *Measure For Measure* (1950) from a photograph by Angus McBean; *The Merry Wives of Windsor* (1911) from *The Illustrated Sporting and Dramatic News*, 4 March 1911; *As You Like It* (1932) from a photograph by Claude Harris in the Birmingham Shakespeare Library; *Much Ado About Nothing* (1898) from a photograph by Ellis and Walery in the Harvard Theatre Collection; and *Twelfth Night* (Ben Greet Company) from *New York Theatre*, April 1904, in the Harvard Theatre Collection.

Preface

This small book is an essay; the first view of a subject about which we were curious. It is based in part on notes set down immediately after performances which we had seen ourselves. Remembering them has been pleasant.

Our collaboration has been close. Chapters One, Three, and Five might have been signed A.C.S., since he was primarily concerned with them, and the personal pronoun, when it is introduced, refers to him. For the same reason the initials J.C.T. might have appeared after Chapters Two, Four, Six, and Seven. We do, however, hold ourselves jointly responsible for all statements of fact. The extent to which examples are cited, or supporting statements quoted, varies greatly. Any temptation to indulge in statistics was, we felt, to be firmly resisted.

A certain amount of fresh research has accompanied the preparation of the book. But although this yielded answers to some of our questions, others remain almost as they stood when we first asked them. What is conventional on the stage today may go back far in time, or only to yesterday. When did Starveling in *A Midsummer Night's Dream* become very old and lose his hearing? Oswald Dale Roberts raised the question in the *Daily Telegraph*, 2 September 1929. Mr Punch had concerned himself with it in December 1905. But neither of them knew, nor as yet do we.

It remains to thank some of the many persons who have

helped us. Among members of the profession, we turned most frequently to the late Mr Allan Wilkie, C.B.E., whose preicse recollection of Shakespearian performances before and soon after the First World War were of inestimable value. Mr Robert Atkins, C.B.E., Mr John Harrison (formerly of the Birmingham Repertory), and Mr George Skillan have been consulted also, more than once. Mr Glen Byam Shaw, C.B.E., and Professor Nevill Coghill have written to us at length about their productions of *As You Like It* and *A Midsummer Night's Dream;* and Mr V. C. Clinton-Baddeley has cleared up an important point concerning revivals of *Troilus and Cressida.* Our debt to librarians is a heavy one, and especially to Miss Waveney Payne, of the Shakespeare Memorial Library, Birmingham; Miss Helen Willard and Miss Jeanne Newlin, of the Harvard Theatre Collection; Miss Eileen Robinson, of the Shakespeare Centre, Stratford-upon-Avon; and Mr Anthony Latham, of the Enthoven Collection, Victoria and Albert Museum, London. We are grateful also to Mr Vincent Pearmain, of the Royal Shakespeare Theatre, for his untiring courtesy.

A.C.S.
J.C.T.

Introduction

I

At least one prominent British dramatist, late in the 1950s, complained that there was too much Shakespeare in the theatre, and that there should be a close season for it. This must have been a personal caprice, for at that time there had been no regular classical company on the road for ten years — since, indeed, Donald Wolfit had ceased to tour — and in London the Old Vic was to give way before long to the National Theatre: six Shakespearian plays in five years instead of half-a-dozen in a single season.

All said, the observation was curiously thoughtless. In his youth the speaker would have had many chances to see Shakespeare; now that he was tired of the plays himself, he might have considered a new generation of playgoers who had never had his fortune.

Certainly, during the early 1920s, a young playgoer in what was technically a Number Two town — taking, that is, the second rank of touring companies — could often count on two Shakespeare weeks in a year. On tour then was the Frank Benson company, with Benson himself in his early sixties but as active as ever. His company was in the last days of its pride, though 'Pa' — as his associates called him, if not to his face — was finding it far harder to get the type of young player that had once made classical history with him. Elsewhere, Henry Baynton, once a Bensonian and later H. B. Irving's understudy, had a redoubtable touring

11

programme; and other companies were led by Charles Doran, Alexander Marsh, and Edward Dunstan. Moreover, certain towns had annual 'festivals' that might be sponsored by the veteran Ben (later Sir Philip Ben) Greet, or by Harold V. Neilson (born Thomas Clegg) who had done much on the classical fringe.

These companies, working on a small budget, kept to a familiar run of plays: among the tragedies, *Macbeth, Hamlet, Romeo and Juliet*, and *Julius Caesar;* among the comedies, *The Merchant of Venice, The Taming of the Shrew, As You Like It, Twelfth Night*, and, less often, *The Merry Wives of Windsor*, though this had seldom been out of Benson's programme in the old days when, as the late Henry Caine said once, a week usually began with 'The Merry Shrews of Venice'.[1] Few histories were toured in the early 1920s except Benson's *Henry V;* and some plays never appeared. Thus *Measure for Measure, The Two Gentlemen of Verona, Love's Labour's Lost, Troilus and Cressida, Timon of Athens, Coriolanus*, and *Cymbeline* were unknown. None of the companies had *Much Ado About Nothing* in its repertory; the play had not been staged in the West End of London since 1905, and one had to seek it at Stratford-upon-Avon — where it was something of a mascot — or, infrequently, at the Old Vic.*

Now and then, but not for long, an adventurous touring manager would try a relative rarity. Baynton, searching for new leading parts, experimented with *King Lear* and, more briefly, with *Antony and Cleopatra*, where his leading lady was Florence Glossop-Harris. He also had *The Comedy of Errors* in his list. The reason was simple. Liking to do *The Bells* on a

*The Shakespearian plays to be seen at this time by audiences in Boston, Massachusetts, were much the same. *Othello* and *King Lear* were among them, however (Lear was a favourite part with the tragedian, Robert B. Mantell), and *Much Ado About Nothing*. We did not have *Henry V*, but were familiar with *Richard III* in Cibber's version. A.C.S.

Saturday night — he had been H. B. Irving's understudy for Mathias — he would begin with a cut version of *The Comedy*, acted without an interval, and with the Dromios in black-face.

In every company, *The Merchant of Venice*, *As You Like It*, *Twelfth Night*, and *Macbeth* were essential, and usually, but not always, *Hamlet*. The texts were so similar that one might have visualized a stock prompt-book. In *Hamlet*, one never had the Polonius–Reynaldo scene; the Dumb Show was cut; the last scene but one began invariably at:

> 'I am very sorry, good Horatio,
> That to Laertes I forgot myself . . .'
>
> (V. ii.75–76).

True, Fortinbras was a rarity: Ben Greet included him when Frank Darch played Hamlet on tour in 1922; but he was missing from the Hamlets of Milton, Marsh, and Baynton. No *Julius Caesar* had the murder of Cinna the poet; the English Doctor in *Macbeth* was unknown. So was the Latin lesson in *The Merry Wives of Windsor* and *The Merchant of Venice*, III. v.: Launcelot, Jessica, Lorenzo. *The Taming of the Shrew* was played without the Induction.

Acting was both downright and down-stage. Speech was full-throated; Baynton and Doran had each a slow, throbbingly sonorous delivery.[2] These productions were Shakespeare of the theatre theatrical. They were fortunate in a central core of actors who, like Kenneth Wicksteed (more than 200 Shakespearian parts), and Edward J. Wood (160), were ready for practically anything. Supporting players could interchange parts at short notice.

Settings varied between the rudimentary and the realistic. Thus, for a *Hamlet* at the old Theatre Royal in Plymouth during the spring of 1922, Ben Greet employed a set of grey curtains that, for the 'platform before the castle', were bunched together as pillars: odd in this particular scene. The same curtains, unbunched, with an old frayed tapestry, a throne, and a chair for Hamlet, served for much of the rest of the play: the Gravedigger had a special tub of earth. In *The Tempest*, Greet represented the storm-tossed ship most satisfactorily by a pole, with a single glimmering red lantern, that swung through a wide arc against a grey curtain. These companies relied upon the local theatre to provide them with a stock Wood or Garden set. Thus Olivia's garden appeared in Plymouth, through the years, with the same formal backcloth of painted box hedges in perspective: a few practicable shrubs were added for the plotters. *As You Like It* was played in cutout trees with a good deal of visible gauze — not that audiences worried about these things — and no manager thought of marking the change to spring from 'winter and rough weather'. *The Merchant of Venice* had, more than once, a gaudy Venetian backcloth that was topographically impossible[3] but never queried.

Benson, Baynton, and Doran varied their sets more than the others, and in late years Baynton toured some of Tree's old scenery, though by this time the fashion for excessive realism had long waned. Benson had a few set-pieces, such as the Orchard in *Romeo and Juliet* where his Juliet (the young American, Genevieve Townsend, whose real name was Smeek) would occupy an ample sculptured marble balcony in the middle of a remarkably arboreal and gauzy garden. Benson made much, also, of the railed Capulet tomb, into which he would break from outside after some hard work with mattock and wrenching-iron. Charles Doran's scenery was more carefully pictorial than those in other companies — some of his sets had been toured in South Africa by Henry Herbert — and he cared more than most managers for his lighting.

Between the scenes either the tableau curtains were closed or the drop-curtain fell. A play had to be chopped up into little pieces, with no attempt whatever to carry it through in a permanent set. Thus Doran staged *Macbeth* with sixteen changes, all noted carefully on the programme, including three scenes in which 'the curtain will fall momentarily to denote the passing of a few hours'.[4] The localities were various: a Barren Place, a Pass, a Lane to the Castle, Corridor in the Castle, the Plain before Dunsinane. Benson, in the following year, 1923, was content with fourteen scenes, ending on the Castle Ramparts. During the next year Harold V. Neilson, presenting Ernest Milton in a so-called 'festival' production, increased the number of scenes to nineteen, setting Banquo's murder in a Wood and ending the tragedy Near Dunsinane. With all these scene-breaks, and an average of three long intervals, the texts had to be firmly cut.

One might have supposed that the companies, as with their prompt-books, drew upon a common stock of costumes. *Hamlet*, invariably was stage-Viking; *Macbeth*, from a Caledonia stern and wild, was what a modern critic has called shaggy-dog; the Athenians of *A Midsummer Night's Dream* were more or less classical Greek. All young men in a company had — as Donald Wolfit said — to provide themselves with accessories: his were black and brown tights, black and brown shoes, two ballet shirts, and a 'half-flow wig'.[5]

Several players among the 'pomping folk' of the time would become celebrated. Charles Doran, an Irishman who had worked with Benson and who was a sound theatrical artificer without pretending to inspiration, had Ralph Richardson and Donald Wolfit (Woolfitt then) in his companies, as well as Edith Sharpe, Neil Porter, Abraham Sofaer, and Norman Shelley. Ernest Milton, already honoured in London, would play Hamlet in a Neilson 'festival' (which meant the stitching together of a few productions rapidly assembled and taken to four or five towns). Compared with today's Shakespeare, it seems in recollection to have been leisurely, conventional, but also dignified and honest. Sometimes, thanks to a special performance, it could flash into genuine excitement. One recalls Milton's Hamlet, Oberon, Ford; the Henry V of

Benson who, when even past sixty, could wear something of
the rose of youth; Genevieve Townsend's Portia and subtly-
phrased Juliet; the young Ariel of Leslie French; certain
speeches — Hamlet's in the Closet scene for instance — by
the handsome Henry Baynton, though he spoiled himself by
becoming an actor-manager too early; and the work of
several of Doran's young men. This was Shakespeare of a
kind we do not get now, intended expressly for a provincial
stage in theatres of plush-and-gilt, cherubs, and caryatids.
Poel and Granville-Barker might never have lived for all the
effect their theories had on the touring practitioners; and in
the mid-twenties one saw barely a sign of the innovations
Robert Atkins had brought to the Old Vic, or any of the fluent
swiftness of Bridges-Adams's work at Stratford-upon-Avon.
Even so, it was always highly professional. It kept to the point,
and Shakespeare was undiminished, except when an occasional low comedian did more than was set down for him.
J.C.T.

II

With such old-fashioned companies, as even more
with the resident companies which they succeeded, tradition
mattered, lending a certain dignity to their art. Had the
present essay been attempted in the 1920s, it would have had
to take account of a far greater number of spectral survivals
from the time of Barry Sullivan and Edwin Booth. That it
was no longer a living tradition is clear enough at this distance.
Even then the enjoyment which one took in a performance
of Charles Doran's company, or, on the other side of the
Atlantic, in that of Robert B. Mantell, was not wholly
without condescension. Would tonight's Richard III really
say:

Off with his head — So much for Buckingham?
One hoped he would.

A quantity of low comic business handed down from the past still disfigured the plays. The Gravedigger, it is true, no longer removed a quantity of assorted waistcoats before beginning his toil on Ophelia's grave. That aberration had lingered in provincial performances down to the early years of the century, but it was gone by now. But Oswald in *King Lear* was still likely to make a ludicrous attack on Kent in the stocks, only to be scared away by the threatening gestures of his enemy; and in *Twelfth Night* Sir Toby and Sir Andrew still indulged in familiar absurdities with their candles and long pipes in what was known as the Kitchen Scene. Very little of this traditional business has lasted. The extravagances and distortions to which the comedies are still at times subjected belong to a different age. There is, too, I should say, a less innocent, or wholehearted enjoyment of the comic scenes in tragedy. That these are not wholly detachable, that our mirth in experiencing them may be checked by a shudder, is now generally recognized. It has been some time since I saw a Gravedigger who aroused, or perhaps wished to arouse, loud and general laughter.

Our present-day reservations about the acceptance of unalloyed comedy in Shakespeare's tragedies may have something to do with the disuse of two long familiar 'doubles', Polonius and one of the Gravediggers (most likely the First) in *Hamlet*, and Peter and the Apothecary in *Romeo and Juliet*.[6] The former was once the most popular of all Shakespearian 'doubles'. I saw Ben Greet play the parts — 'Corambis' and 'Clown', as they were called — in his First Quarto *Hamlet* at Jordan Hall, Boston, 9 December 1929. Both combinations presume the sort of specialization which went on in the old stock companies where the players were cast according to their various 'lines of business'; as 'heavies', say, or Old Men, soubrettes, or ingénues. The Nurse's man, Peter, and the Gravedigger were made to order for the principal Low Comedian; but so, as the rôles had come to be regarded, were the Apothecary and, I regret to say, Polonius. Today, the Apothecary is more sinister, or pitiful, than humorous, while Polonius admits a variety of interpretation but tends to be associated with the corruption of an evil court.

Indeed, I can think of only one double which has persisted from an earlier time. In *Richard II* the combining of the Duke of Norfolk, who disappears early, with the Bishop of Carlisle, who appears late, is still associated with the Benson company, and especially Oscar Asche. In the season of 1929–30, however, it was used both at the Old Vic (with Donald Wolfit) and by the Stratford company on tour in America; and in 1955 and 1956 it turns up at the Old Vic (Robert Hardy), the Birmingham Repertory Theatre, and the Citizens' Theatre, Glasgow. Equally familiar to us is the doubling of the Ghost and First Player in *Hamlet:* so familiar, indeed, that we might be tempted to suppose that it was of very early origin. But there is, in point of fact, little trace of it before the 1930s, when Mark Dignam twice assumed the two rôles. He has had many successors.

The relaxing of what were once fixed practices is observable in this matter of doubling, as, equally, the fact that in occasional instances custom still holds. Much the same is true of the scenic backgrounds and indications of place. One no longer expects to see bridges, practicable or otherwise, in *The Merchant of Venice;* or a complete chapel for the wedding of Romeo and Juliet — though one may catch a glimpse of the lovers kneeling before an altar. The Forest of Arden is usually unencumbered with trees. On this last point, I turned for information, as so often before, to my friend Allan Wilkie, an actor who headed his own touring company in Great Britain before 1914 and again in Australia soon after the war. In reply he wrote:

> A large tree set R.C. in the forest scene in 'As You' on which Orlando hung his verses and on a log set in front of which Jaques sat for the delivery of his famous speech

was very traditional, and I never remember taking part in or seeing a production of 'As You' that was otherwise.

In Michael Elliott's production at Stratford in 1961 a big oak, bare of leaves at the beginning, for it was then winter, stood at the top of a sort of knoll throughout the play. It served many purposes.

Within memory, one scene in a play of Shakespeare's has been newly located, by means, chiefly, of a single property. When Hamlet after the Play Scene is summoned to his mother's 'closet', it would have been, in Shakespeare's meaning of the word, to a private room merely.[7] There is nothing in the lines to indicate that it is a bedchamber, and indeed the only mention of a bed is of the King's bed, which is certainly elsewhere. In the staging of the scene a chair is conspicuous in early pictures, as in the famous one accompanying the tragedy in Rowe's edition (1709). In the 1920s an austere couch or sofa is added to the chair, as with the Baynton company on its provincial tours and in the Barrymore and Kingsway productions. Meanwhile, critical interest in the sexual and even Freudian aspects of the play has been mounting. It is in keeping that what used to be known as the Closet Scene becomes 'the Bedroom Scene' in Dover Wilson's *What Happens in Hamlet* (1935). An actual bed, predictably, was introduced in Gielgud's brilliant *Hamlet* in New York the next year. (Earlier, in London, the actor had suggested one, by means of curtains.[8]) By 1950 Mr Kenneth Tynan was wondering '*why* there should be a bed centre stage in every production of this scene. It is never mentioned and never slept in.'[9] A.C.S.

III

Round most of the plays was a coral reef of selected tradition that had grown steadily through the years. Sir Tyrone Guthrie has held that 'what we of the 20th century

have inherited is not a Shakespearian tradition; it is merely a
legacy of 19th century conventions'.[10] But Sir Tyrone may
not have asked whence many of these conventions derived
and why thay have persisted. 'Tradition', said Granville-
Barker, 'is so strong in the theatre that a historian may really
be advised to write its history backwards.'[11]

Even today, when directors dislike doing the same things
twice,[12] the most reasonable of the old customs and traditions
linger because they help actor and audience and do no violence
to the play. Actors have known instinctively which points to
choose from other performances and which to drop. Directors
as well. A good revival of *Much Ado About Nothing* (London,
1969) used a few devices that will certainly be transient: the
setting, for example, in a tennis-court of the scene that de-
velops to Don John's accusation. No doubt the director,
seeking a change, had caught at the line, 'The old ornament
of his cheek hath already stuffed tennis-balls' (III. iii. 41–42).
Yet even in this contemporary production some of the phra-
sing and business rested on tradition, however much it had
been varied: the handling of the first Watch scene, and the
business with the goblets when Dogberry and Verges called
on Leonato before the wedding. The Arbour scene had its
fresh adornments — a Boy became an under-gardener — but
the general pattern, the emphases, were familiar. Don John
(see Chapter Five) wore black.

In the light of history, the productions that survive — other
than curiosities — are the most logical. Shakespeare production, like anything else, must flower, and has flowered;
but the old is there, mingled with the new. 'Tis in grain; 'twill
endure wind and weather. To this day, in revival upon revival,
one can discern — whatever the apparent differences — the
outlines (like ancient 'lynchets' seen in an air photograph) of
the Shakespeare productions that Benson, Doran, and the
rest were touring nearly half a century ago. J.C.T.

CHAPTER ONE

Stage Business

As one reviews the progress of Shakespearian studies since the close of the First World War, certain approaches can be seen to have been far more profitable than others. An understanding of the ideas of order accepted by the Elizabethans proved more illuminating, for instance, than the attempt to apply their conflicting notions of the nature of melancholy. The isolation of themes, through the presence of repeated images, was not wasted effort, though it might lead, unhappily, to forgetfulness of the artistic medium in which Shakespeare worked and even of the rich humanity of what he achieved.

The approach to the plays merely as plays led to a closer examination of the text itself, in which, as we now perceive, so much is concentrated that as we read we become aware of the faces of the characters, their actions, and gestures. This is accomplished, furthermore, largely without the aid of stage directions, the lines themselves serving as something like a dramatic score. Among recent writers who have done most to advance such knowledge I mention the Swiss scholar, Professor Rudolf Stamm, and John Russell Brown, of the University of Birmingham.

The dependence of certain lines on the action which accompanies them was so obvious as to have forced itself, quite early, upon the attention of Shakespearian scholars. Polonius, after reminding the King of the accuracy of certain statements in the past, bids him:

Take this from this if this be otherwise (II. ii. 155)

and his gesture shows that the first 'this' refers to his head, the second to his shoulders, and the third to his news. The line is unintelligible without its accompaniment. Less certainly right, though for practical purposes right enough, is Launcelot Gobbo's business of kneeling with his back toward that dim-witted, dim-sighted, true-begotten father of his, who, stroking the young man's long hair, is astonished by what he takes to be the luxuriance of his beard. This time it is possible to imagine a different explanation given to the passage (the use, say, of a cap and long plume) but scarcely one which would be as convincing. Or there is the incompleteness of Richard the Second's words as Bolingbroke kneels to him in the shadows of the base court of Flint Castle:

Up, cousin, up! Your heart is up, I know,
Thus high at least.

Here although there is no question of the meaning which his gesture imparts to 'thus high', there is doubt about the gesture itself. Richard is suggesting that Henry seeks his crown; but is he wearing a crown as he speaks, and pointing to it, or merely circling his brow with a movement of the hand? From Holinshed it seems clear that Richard assumed as much dignity as he could at this moment, and had the sword of state carried before him as he entered. In a popular theatre, moreover, a King would be likely to wear his crown at all times unless there was reason for his not doing so. What matters is not, however, which action is chosen, both are current on our stage, but that one or the other is demanded by the text.

So far, the examples of incompleteness, of lines in need of action to clarify their meaning, have been self-evident. The actors cast as Polonius and young Gobbo can only be doing at these moments what their Elizabethan counterparts did; the actor cast as Richard cannot go far astray. A last example

stands somewhat apart. Action is clearly demanded by
character and situation alike, but it is less clearly reflected in
the lines. The Nurse has come to Romeo to receive a message
from him for her mistress.

ROMEO. Bid her devise
　　Some means to come to shrift this afternoon;
　　And there she shall at Friar Laurence' cell
　　Be shriv'd and married. Here is for thy pains.
NURSE. No, truly, sir; not a penny.
ROMEO. Go to! I say you shall.
NURSE. This afternoon, sir? Well, she shall be there.
ROMEO. And stay good nurse . . . (II. iv. 74)

and he gives her further instructions. What is not told us is
that after a weak pretence of disinterestedness, she takes the
money. 'Nurse *looking a contrary way, takes the purse*' is a satis-
factory stage direction here.[1] No nurse, conceivably, has
ever held out long.

　　Stage business of a more exciting sort, not called for by the
text but the invention of actors, occurs at certain awaited
moments in the plays. The experienced theatregoer is well
acquainted with these. What, he wonders, will tonight's
Hamlet or Shylock or Richard III do when he reaches
such and such a line. Audiences in the time of the Kembles
and Edmund Kean asked much the same questions, attaching
to them, however, a much greater importance than we do.
(Emphasis on the actor's conception of his part, rather than
on 'points', began only with the performances of Macready.)

　　Hamlet, not surprisingly, contains several of these moments
and I have chosen one of them as illustration.[2] In the impas-
sioned soliloquy at the close of Act Two Hamlet cries out
against the evil King:

　　　Bloody, bawdy villain!
　　Remorseless, treacherous, kindless villain!
　　O, vengeance!

then checking himself:

> Why, what an ass am I! This is most brave,
> That I, the son of a dear father murther'd,
> Prompted to my revenge by heaven and hell,
> Must like a whore unpack my heart with words
> And fall a-cursing like a very drab,
> A scullion!

In 1936 when American audiences were comparing with much interest the Hamlets of John Gielgud and Leslie Howard, it was noticeable that the former merely drew his dagger at the climax, whereas Howard frantically thrust at the King's throne as if to stab its occupant to death. This business, which goes back at least to Beerbohm Tree, has not disappeared, but it has been varied repeatedly. So within the last ten years I have seen the Prince drive his dagger into a table (John Neville); beat with his hands on the seat of the throne (Richard Hampton); tear to pieces the Player's manuscript containing the Hecuba speech (Ian Bannen); break the Player's wooden sword (Giorgio Albertazzi); overturn and then replace the throne chair (David Warner); and kick down the throne chair from the dais (Richard Pasco). It is not, however, for any absurdity of action that Hamlet is blaming himself but for empty protestation, words without deeds. The more violent inventions, therefore, though they may suit the mood of the speaker, are out of keeping with what he says, and those actors (and there are a fair number) who dispense with business altogether seem likeliest to be fulfilling the author's intention.[3]

Most of such stage business as survives from the past originated in the 19th century, but in a few cases (a very few) it is older, going back seemingly to Shakespeare's own time. In a minor work of 1607, Sharpham's comedy *The Fleire*, mention is made of one who 'Like *Thisbe* in the play' almost killed himself with 'the scabberd'. That Pyramus should so literally fall on his sword that Thisby is unable to find it, or only with help from the deceased, is familiar enough. But though a desperate recourse to the empty scabbard as a weapon of death is not unknown in performances nowadays, it is very unusual.

Macbeth, on the other hand, in the Banquet Scene, raises his cup to toast, 'our dear friend Banquo, whom we miss./ Would he were here' . . . then lets it drop, or dashes it to the ground, upon the Ghost's return. And this business is glanced at in the last act of *The Knight of the Burning Pestle* (*c.* 1607), when Jasper disguised as a ghost threatens Venturewell. He will visit him even when he is at table among his friends.

> I'll come in midst of all thy pride and mirth,
> Invisible to all men but thyself,
> And whisper such a sad tale in thine ear
> Shall make thee let the cup fall from thy hand,
> And stand as mute and pale as death itself.

There must, I suppose, have been an occasional Macbeth who as he addressed the Ghost,

> Avaunt, and quit my sight! Let the earth hide thee!

carefully replaced his glass on the table; but if so he was scarcely suiting the action to the word.

Macbeth's business, which is referred to several times about the middle of the 18th century,[4] is as natural as it is traditional. In two other instances, one from *Othello*, one from *Hamlet*, stage business still familiar today is traceable to a time as early as that of the great Betterton (1635–1710), an actor whose Hamlet, we are told, endeavoured to reproduce a still earlier, Jacobean interpretation of the part.

In *Othello* the business which I have in mind comes in the great third act when the Moor, doubting for an instant the truth of what he has heard, lays hold of Iago, half-throttling him, or flinging him to the ground:

> Villain, be sure thou prove my love a whore!
> Be sure of it . . . (III. iii. 363).

The sudden shift to action here is striking. It is often referred to in the 18th century, and gave a name to the scene in which it occurs, which came to be known as 'The Collaring Scene'. In Nicholas Rowe's edition of Shakespeare (1709) the stage direction at this point is *'Catching hold on him'*; and still earlier, in Otway's *Don Carlos* (1676), a tragedy in which the relationship between Philip II and the villainous Rui-Gomez is very much like that between Othello and Iago, and Shakespeare's tragedy is many times echoed, the King turning all at once upon his tormentor *'seizes roughly on* Rui-Gomez'. Betterton, it is worth noting, was Philip in this play and conceivably used here the same business he was accustomed to use in *Othello*. That this is not absolutely necessary to the interpretation of the passage, its meaning, and movement, is I suppose true. In the theatre its rightness seems incontestable.

In *Hamlet*, traditional business accompanies the lines addressed to Gertrude beginning,

> Look here upon this picture, and on this,
> The counterfeit presentment of two brothers,

as the Prince forces her to examine actual miniatures ('pictures in little') of the old King and the new. So he was accustomed to do through much of the 18th century if not before. Against his use of miniatures — and the passage has been long debated — only one piece of evidence is of much weight. In Rowe's Shakespeare is an engraving of the Closet Scene at the moment of the Ghost's return. Several details suggest that the artist was remembering the play as he had seen it acted. And on the wall two large half-length portraits are partly visible, those presumably of the two kings. Hamlet, it is urged, had only to point at one of these as he spoke. But because some details in the engraving are theatrical in origin it does not follow that all must be. An illustrator of the scene might have been tempted to introduce the pictures, regardless of what was done on the stage. And one further detail, long overlooked, is curious. For Gertrude is certainly wearing a chain, on which is suspended what appears to be a locket, the locket containing, we may suppose, that picture in little of Claudius which Hamlet will snatch from her a moment later, to contrast with that of his father.[5]

Other pieces of business, much used in the past and still extant, include a neat device in *King John*. As the battle begins in that rarely given play, Faulconbridge meets and kills, off-stage, his father's enemy the Duke of Austria. He returns carrying Austria's severed head.

> Now, by my life, this day grows wondrous hot!
> Some airy devil hovers in the sky
> And pours down mischief. Austria's head lie there
> While Philip breathes —

and he flings down his burden. As John Philip Kemble rearranged the passage in his acting edition (1814). Faulconbridge speaks the first three lines, through 'pours down mischief', as soliloquy. Austria enters, they fight, and Faulconbridge drives him from the stage; only to return, no longer with the head but with the distinctive lion's skin worn by his foe. This arrangement not only provides a bit of desirable single combat but also gets rid of a property too often laughed at when it is shown. Sometimes, indeed, all reference to the head is now omitted. I once heard 'Austria lie thou there' spoken at this point, instead of 'Austria's head lie there'; and in a Stratford promptbook of 1940 'head' is ingeniously emended to 'hyde'.

Our first sight of Sir John Falstaff is accompanied by the following dialogue:

FALSTAFF. Now Hal, what time of day is it, lad?

> PRINCE. Thou art so fat-witted with drinking of old sack,
> and unbuttoning thee after supper, and sleeping
> upon benches after noon, that thou hast forgotten to
> ask that truly which thou wouldest truly know
> (*I Henry IV*, I. ii. 1).

It is noteworthy that in 1804 Stephen Kemble (the big, as distinguished from his brother, the great Kemble) appearing as Falstaff in Manchester was praised in *The Townsman*, 16 June, for a new idea: 'the discovery of Falstaff on a Couch, in his first scene, as if awaking'. This was much preferred by the critics to 'the common method of walking on, from opposite sides', since it gave point to the Knight's question. The idea reappears in the 20th century. I saw Falstaff awakened from slumber in Margaret Webster's production, with Maurice Evans as Sir John, at the Forrest Theatre, Philadelphia, 17 December, 1937, and at Jasper Deeter's excellent Hedgerow Theatre, in the spring of 1940, with Harry Sheppard. In 1946 the business took on a new dignity. In that year, Dover Wilson, an editor unusual in his recognition of the fact that Shakespeare's plays were designed to be acted, having just read about Stephen Kemble's idea, used it as the basis for a stage direction in the New Cambridge Edition. 'The point of this has eluded the critics', he wrote of the opening words of the scene. 'A "discovery" of Fal. asleep (behind the curtains of the inner stage) would provide one and is suggested in ll. 4–5.' At Stratford, five years later, when under Dover Wilson's influence the histories from *Richard II* to *Henry V* were given in sequence, one of the few discoveries used was at this moment, when Hal descending from the gallery roused his fat companion by flinging a boot against the curtain to the inner stage. The same, or similar, business has been used in a number of subsequent productions.

Perpetuated from the Kemble time to ours is another idea: that Viola on landing in Illyria should have luggage. Why

this is thought necessary I find hard to understand. Viola asks
the Captain to conceal her identity;

> and be my aid
> For such disguise as haply shall become
> The form of my intent (*Twelfth Night*, I. ii. 53).

Later she says that she imitated the fashion of her brother's
clothes, not that she wore them (III. iv. 366). The fortuitously
preserved trunk raises more questions than it answers. In
other Shakespearian plays as well, the arrival or departure of
travellers is marked by the appearance of staggering porters.
Our liking for stage luggage has become excessive. Chests
and boxes are not inappropriately introduced, it may be,
when Bertram is setting out for Paris, or Valentine for Milan,
or even when Othello and his bride are landing in Cyprus.
But to have Hamlet furnished with a trunk, as he is about to
leave for England, simply will not do — if only because a
playgoer of any imagination begins wondering who packed it
and what it contains.

Two pieces of business in *Othello*, one realistic, the other,
I am afraid, melodramatic, have descended to use from the
middle of the last century. The first seems to have been
introduced by Charles Dillon in 1856. It supplies a background for the beginning of the central scene in the tragedy,
as Iago opens his attack upon the Moor himself.

> IAGO. My noble lord.
> OTHELLO. What dost thou say, Iago?
> IAGO. Did Michael Cassio, when you woo'd my lady,
>   Know of your love?
> OTHELLO. He did, from first to last. Why dost thou ask?

The pauses in the dialogue imply, it would seem, some pre-
occupation on Othello's part. Iago's words, only half heard
at the outset, interrupt him in something he is doing. That he
should have sat down, just before, to examine official papers,

or perhaps a plan of the fortification, while Iago, acting for
the moment as secretary, stands behind him, gains this
effect perfectly. An imaginative variation, a good idea in a
production in which good ideas were not numerous (Tony
Richardson's at Stratford in 1959) set Iago to work, as they
talked, polishing and sharpening Othello's sword. But the
business with the papers is usual.

The scene of attempted assassination is, like that of the
murder of Banquo, notoriously difficult to play through,
without laughter. Why this is so, I am at a loss to explain.
Possibly Iago's hypocrisy has something to do with it.
Sometimes, too, the scene is thrust forward, in the staging,
and deprived of depth. Often the lighting is at fault, neither
bright enough for intelligibility nor dark enough for illusion.
As for the business with which we are concerned, it implies a
heavily cut acting edition.

In the full text Iago makes off after the wounding of Cassio
and Roderigo, who cry for help. Othello appears briefly.
Satisfied that Iago has carried out his part of their compact,
he goes to fulfil his own. Lodovico and Gratiano enter, but
they fear an ambush and do not immediately come forward.
Iago, as if just aroused from sleep, returns, carrying a torch.
He goes at once to Cassio's assistance, calling on the others
to do so. Then, discovering Roderigo, he stabs him as one of
his friend's assailants.

> IAGO. Kill men i' th' dark? Where be these bloody
> thieves? How silent is this town! Ho! murther!
> murther!

Now as early as the Kemble edition of 1814, Othello's part
in the scene is omitted, as it is regularly omitted today, and
the entrance of Lodovico and Gratiano is delayed, so that
Iago, returning with his torch almost immediately, is alone
with the wounded men. He stabs Roderigo. Here was introduced the new business, attributed to the American tragedian,

Edwin Booth. For Cassio is still alive, and standing over his body the villain is about to make sure of him too ('How silent is this town') when he hears Lodovico and Gratiano approaching and sets up his cry of murther. With the abridged text this action is conceivable enough. Its sensationalism commended it, no doubt, at the beginning, but it has had a long history. Irving used it, as well as Booth, and I have seen it a half-dozen times, most notably at the Forrest Theatre, Philadelphia, 25 December 1936, when Brian Aherne was the Iago, and at Stratford in the productions of Godfrey Tearle in 1949 and Anthony Quayle in 1954.

A final instance of business carried over from the past comes from near the close of the last century. In the fifth scene of *Hamlet* there is a clear pause following the Ghost's last words of admonition and farewell. Then Hamlet:

> O all you host of heaven! O earth! What else?
> And shall I couple hell? Hold, hold, my heart!
> And you, my sinews, grow not instant old,
> But bear me stiffly up.

In his review of Forbes-Robertson's *Hamlet* in the *Manchester Guardian*, 23 May 1898, Oliver Elton noted 'as a subtle and attentive point (if we read it right)' the actor's 'lying exhausted and supine', after the Ghost's revelation, and 'looking up at the stars' to give meaning to his apostrophe, 'O all you host of heaven'.[6] I remember John Barrymore's employing the same action in the mid-1920s and how exciting it seemed to me then — and how right too (I am a little less certain of its rightness now). Among other actors to use it, and there have been many, Donald Wolfit was perhaps the next in time.[7]

Turning now from business originating several generations ago to business traceable only within the span of our own years of playgoing, we encounter difficulties still. Much of current theatrical criticism quite ignores detail. I am uncertain, for instance, just when Mercutio in teasing the Nurse —

> An old hare hoar,
> And an old hare hoar,
> Is very good meat in Lent —

added the outrage of snatching at her skirts. I saw this done in Laurence Olivier's production at the Fifty-First Street Theatre, New York, 10 May 1940, when May Whitty was the indignant Angelica; and I have seen it often since, right down to the Zeffirelli film. But how early is it? Not as early, I think, as the first years of the century, when the impropriety of the attempt might have been too pronounced. A better guess would be the Old Vic sometime in the twenties or thirties — but this is a guess only.

For contrast, another device, current today, is as clearly vouched for as could be desired. This business might be called 'The Theft of the King's Sword'. It comes in the Prayer Scene in *Hamlet*. Claudius as he kneels to pray lays aside his sword. Hamlet, entering behind him, takes possession of it. It is this sword which he addresses at the climax of his soliloquy.

> Up, sword, and know thou a more horrid hent,

and with it, later, he stabs Polonius to death. As the King rises he misses the sword.

Sir John Gielgud takes pride in this device, which he introduced at the New Theatre in 1934 and used many times subsequently. A practical argument in its favour is that it relieves the actor from carrying a sword in the Play Scene, where it is awkward for him, and furnishes him with one in the Closet Scene, where one is necessary. The business has been popular with actors. Gielgud brought it to America in 1936. Tom Rutherfurd used it in Bridgeport, Connecticut, in 1945; Schofield at Stratford in 1948; Redgrave for the Old Vic in 1949; and Burton, under Gielgud's direction, in New York in 1964. It figured also in several of Michael Benthall's productions, and in one of these (by the Old Vic Company

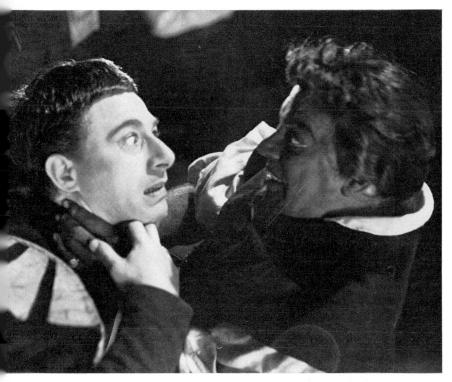

1. 'VILLAIN, BE SURE THOU PROVE MY LOVE A WHORE'
Douglas Campbell as Othello and Paul Rogers as Iago, Old Vic,
1951.

facing page 32]

2. THE PARTING OF HASTINGS AND JANE SHORE

Richmond, Surrey, Shakespeare Society in *Richard III*, 1966:
Marian Huggett as Jane, John Oliver as Hastings, Jim Stack as
Catesby.

at the Broadway Theatre in 1959) I remember the King's
rushing out at the close of the scene bawling 'My lords! my
lords!' or something of the sort.

It is possible to admire the brilliance of the contrivance
here — as it might be in a well-made, romantic play — and
at the same time to accept it only with reluctance. For these
doings engross our attention, whether at the moment of
Hamlet's securing the weapon or that of the King's finding it
gone, and to the extent that this occurs we no longer con-
centrate on the momentous inner drama which is played out
in the course of the scene. There is, furthermore, the contrast
in styles. Shakespeare's scene is one of extreme formality.
Soliloquy follows soliloquy. Hamlet's is spoken in the presence
of the man whose life or death is being debated. The King's,
stranger still, reverses the practice of real life, since Claudius
speaks when he would have been silent, then is silent when he
should be uttering the words of a prayer. Gielgud's business, I
cannot help feeling, belongs to a different kind of drama; or,
at least to a different part of this ever-changing play.

Two or three pieces of comic business from *A Midsummer
Night's Dream* and *The First Part of King Henry the Fourth*,
complete this small collection. Lysander and Hermia have
fallen asleep in the wood and Puck, mistaking Lysander for
Demetrius, casts a spell upon him. Waking, he sees Helena
and now loves her. The play's confusions are beginning:

> HELENA. But who is here? Lysander! on the ground?
>   Dead or asleep? I see no blood, no wound.
>   Lysander, if you live, good sir, awake.
> LYSANDER. And run through fire I will for thy sweet sake.
>   Transparent Helena! Nature shows art,
>   That through thy bosom makes me see thy heart.[8]

When, as will be told in a later chapter, the lovers in this play
became figures of fun it was discovered that a point could be
made of Helena's obtuseness here. She no longer understood

3

the compliment to her beauty but with an air of startled modesty hastily drew together the folds of her dress. I first saw her do this at Stratford under Benthall's direction in 1949; next, at Regent's Park, under Robert Atkins, two years later. A variation on what by that time was the established business was introduced at the Old Vic in December 1960, when Robert Muller in the *Daily Mail* complained of the excessive literalness of Michael Langham's direction: 'At "transparent Helena" . . . Helena must perforce look behind her.'⁹

The remaining bits of business are from the Second Tavern Scene (III. iii) in *Henry IV*. They come where business is always likely to be found: at the beginning of the scene, when it is discovered; and at the end, when this is marked by a curtain or blackout. Falstaff, as the scene opens, is concerned a little improbably at his loss of weight:

> Bardolph, am I not fall'n away vilely since this last action? Do I not bate? Do I not dwindle? Why, my skin hangs about me like an old lady's loose gown! I am withered like an old apple-john. . . .

Bardolph takes a gloomy view: 'Sir John, you are so fretful you cannot live long.' In a performance at the Hollis Street Theatre, Boston, by what was then called 'The Stratford-on-Avon Festival Company', under Bridges-Adams, Bardolph was acting as his master's valet and was polishing his belt. His attempt to lengthen it was, I think, the subtlety of a later time. George Skillan has this stage direction in French's Acting Edition of the play (1938):

> Bardolph *sits* R. *of the table mending a sword belt, using a steel needle about three inches long. He is sewing a strip into one that he has found, to make it longer.*

This belt of Falstaff's was still receiving attention in a good performance out-of-doors by the Richmond Shakespeare Society, 12 August 1952.

As the scene draws to a close its mood takes on seriousness. The Prince's final couplet has its trumpet notes. But Falstaff has his couplet too.

> PRINCE. The land is burning; Percy stands on high;
> And either they or we must lower lie.
> *[Exit.]*
> FALSTAFF. Rare words! brave world! Hostess, my break-
> fast, come.
> O, I could wish this tavern were my drum.

It was a characteristic stroke of Margaret Webster's, in her production at the Forrest Theatre, Philadelphia, 17 December 1937, that we were allowed to see Mrs Quickly bring in the breakfast. On 11 May 1946, the Old Vic Company was using the same business at the Century Theatre, New York, the meal this time consisting of an immense steaming pasty in a pewter covered dish. Then came a variation. For in the Brattle Theatre Company's production at the New York Civic Theatre, 1 October 1955, Falstaff, upon removing the cover, found only a single, very small egg. Thus had business once amusing degenerated into silliness.[10]

CHAPTER TWO

Cutting the Text

It is, we must suppose, every Shakespearian's ambition to meet all the plays in performance. Yet, when that is achieved — not an easy task, but easier than it used to be, now that *Titus Andronicus* has proved once more to be actable — another goal remains: to hear spoken from the stage every line the dramatist wrote. This is infinitely harder. It needs a close memory, great patience, and the co-operation of such a director as the late W. Bridges-Adams whom Sir Philip Ben Greet, in a public speech, once called 'Unabridges'. Greet himself — certainly no more than Frank Benson — was not remarkable for his textual fidelity. Today, though simplified staging and a swifter tempo cause acting texts, in general, to be far fuller than they were, certain scenes continue to be elusive; even if we seem to be on target, there is often a nagging realization that the director has cut ten, twenty, thirty lines.*

Textual fidelity was ignored for so long that unspecialized audiences became thoroughly confused. The most notorious perversions are in the common 18th- and 19th-century promptbooks of *Richard III* which were either the work of Colley Cibber or with a strong admixture of his text. Later there must have been a bridge period when a listener to Shakespeare's original play would have sworn that it had

---

* The search must still go on; our ears must stay hopefully alert.

been cut. Where were such flamboyant accretions as 'Off with his head — so much for Buckingham!' and 'A weak invention of the enemy'?*

On the other side, there is a true story of an experienced English actor, early in the 20th century, who had known Shakespeare from a study of the inconsiderable parts allotted to him, and from nothing else. He could not believe, on being faced with an 'entirety' *Hamlet*, that some other hand had not padded out the original. Probably, of all the plays, *Hamlet* has been varied most. To get it into three hours, with the elaborate scenic changes that meant so much cutting, was a problem any manager had to solve as best he could. When Frank Benson gave the whole text at Stratford in the spring of 1899, he decided to take it in two sections, going in the afternoon to the end of the Play Scene, and at night beginning with the King's prayer.[1] The company, having to spatchcock into the text rare speeches and usually cancelled lines, had never been more nervous. In the event the performance was less complete than Benson had hoped: young Matheson Lang, as Voltimand, forgot his long and intricate report and muttered merely its first and last lines:

> Most fair return of greetings and desires
> As therein are set down.

Until Forbes-Robertson's London revival in 1897 it had been the custom to omit Fortinbras. This meant the loss of IV. iv and Hamlet's 'How all occasions' soliloquy. Often a night closed on 'The rest is silence'. Beerbohm Tree (1892) preferred to end with Horatio's 'Flights of angels sing thee to thy rest'. At this moment, according to Clement Scott,[2] an angelic choir was heard faintly to echo the phrase, 'Good night, sweet Prince' — something that 'visibly affected the

---

* These, with other Cibber lines, have had the dignity of inclusion in the *Oxford Book of Quotations*.

audience assembled with hearts full and nerves a little over-strained'. Nowadays, though Fortinbras is reinstated (and Benson himself kept him after the 1899 experiment), we do not invariably have the English Ambassadors. With some reason they were cut from a version in Victorian costume at Stratford in 1948. That year it was a local jest in the company to ask what Queen Victoria and the Prince Consort might have done on receiving an order from Denmark to murder Rosen-crantz and Guildenstern.

The pair have usually survived — though they were cut from the Olivier film (1948) — but we seldom meet Volti-mand and Cornelius, Ambassadors to Norway. Reynaldo, Polonius's servant and his unofficial ambassador to Paris, is also doubtful: Martin Harvey retained some of the part, and those who saw Reynaldo played in full by young Alec Guinness in Tyrone Guthrie's revival at the Old Vic and Elsinore (1937) must always regret his absence from a pro-gramme. Harcourt Williams said in 1935: 'As a distinguished critic wrote the other day, the less that is cut of *Hamlet* the shorter it seems. Having produced the full version I should never be as deeply interested in a cut one, nor can I understand anyone who has seen the complete play wanting anything less.'[3]

Certain scenes and speeches have nearly always suffered in variations of the short text. In touring companies between the wars one never heard Marcellus's 'And now, sit down, and tell me he that knows' (I. i), Hamlet's 'This heavy-headed revel east and west' (I. iv), the central lines of the Ghost's speech ('whose effect . . . all my smooth body') in I. v, the 'aery of children, little eyases' in II. ii — a topical passage that reappeared at Stratford during 1970 — the Dumb Show, much of the King and Laertes in IV. vii, and practically all of the duologue for Hamlet and Horatio at the opening of V. ii. Modern directors, with more time, make their own patterns; but these are still the passages first endangered.

Generally, in a short version, Hamlet keeps all his soliloquies; the King and Laertes lose more than any of the other principals. An unexpected cut in Tony Richardson's production, with Nicol Williamson's resolutely prose Hamlet, at the Roundhouse, London (1969) was the Second Gravedigger: the first time in London's recent memory[4] that we had lost the most familiar of stage riddles. At Stratford in 1958 the second man was described as a Sacristan, a haughty young fellow not a little condescending to the Gravedigger and put out at being sent to Yaughan's for a stoup of liquor.

Hamlet is the longest of the plays. Even the briefest of the tragedies, *Macbeth*, seldom gets through without cuts. Probably the Hecate couplets in III. v ('Have I not reason, beldams as you are . . .?') are, of all Shakespearian speeches, the rarest. The part was once retained for the sake of the Locke music in which Hecate was chief soloist; and, remarkably, it has been doubled with Duncan; probably the last recorded instance was at the Theatre Royal, Glasgow, in October 1874.[5] In February 1869 at Birmingham, and in April 1870 at the Boston Museum, Mrs Howard Paul actually doubled Hecate with Lady Macbeth: she appeared in Boston 'with gauze wings, fair hair waving and streaming into a cloud, and various emblems of incantation woven picturesquely into the costume.'[6] Charles Doran, an Old Bensonian who became an actor-manager, used to keep Hecate in his touring version nearly half a century ago: a major witch, lit in crimson, she was an actress named Gwevril Thomas.[7]

In most *Macbeth* programmes of our time the name is a collector's piece. On Hecate's last notable appearance, so fine an actress as Adéle Dixon played the part in a very full version directed by Andrew Leigh (Old Vic, 1929); she was praised for her work in a 'minor but difficult character'.[8] By 1930 Hecate had gone from the Vic: Harcourt Williams, then director, had a programme note: 'As an experiment, and on reasonable authority, Act I, Scene ii is omitted, together with the doubtful introduction of Hecate. The omission of the "King's Evil" is not so defensible, but expedient.' Hecate is now unloved, and regarded as spurious; even so, for those who hope to capture the entire Folio, her dismissal can be tantalising. So, too, is that of the English Doctor in the 'King's Evil' passage, a compliment to James the First (IV. iii). When Lewis Casson included the passage (Princes, 1926), James Agate could discover 'no earthly reason for its retention',[9] and Hubert Griffith found it not only 'apropos nothing in the story', but coming 'at the worst moment of the drama to hold up the action and mystify everybody'.[10] The scene appeared in the 'Christian' *Macbeth*, directed by Peter Hall, with Paul Scofield, at Stratford in 1967; and, five years before this, Oliver Neville included it in his Old Vic production. G. K. Hunter, in his 1967 edition of *Macbeth*, emphasizes[11] that the report of Edward the Confessor's virtues is used 'to establish the potency of virtuous kingship in our minds before the play plunges on to demonstrate the fate of vicious kingship (and queenship). The episode of Edward's "touching" for "the Evil" (scrofula) seems to have been written, indeed, to link the play's sense of royal virtue with James.' Quoting

> To the succeeding royalty he leaves
> The healing benediction

Professor Hunter adds: 'By the date of the play James had begun, after some hesitation, to "touch" for the King's Evil.' One or two other small but exasperating cuts have been made simply to avoid extending a cast, though it is rare nowadays that we lose Old Siward's epitaph on his son (V. viii), 'Why, then, God's soldier be he'. On a provincial tour, Ross's talk with the Old Man (II. iv) was often sacrificed. In Andrew Leigh's 1928 production at the Old Vic the Old Man was described unexpectedly as 'Steward to Macbeth'.

Now, accustomed to full texts, we can be astonished at

what older playgoers never heard, Often, of course, there were revivals that included more of the play than one would have imagined because minor characters were run together — forming what Arthur Machen, the novelist, who was transiently a Bensonian, called 'a conglomerate or pudding-stone part'. We had late examples of this in the *Antony and Cleopatra* directed by Michael Benthall for Laurence Olivier (St James's 1951), and in a revival of the same play, directed by Robert Helpmann (Old Vic, 1957). In each of these were characters named Philo Canidius, Scarus Dercetas, Alexas Diomedes, and Euphronius Lamprius. Yet each revival omitted various small parts, particularly Antony's general, Ventidius, and the scene (III. i) in which the body of Pacorus of Parthia is borne in triumph across the Syrian plain. Ventidius has been in and out through the century: omitted by Benson at the Lyceum, London, in 1900; usually in at the Old Vic; omitted at Stratford in 1927 and 1945, included during 1935 and 1953.[12]

Though it would take too long to catalogue every cut, here are some of the characters we are always glad to find upon a programme: the Clown (*Othello*), A Roman and a Volscian (Nicanor and Adrian) in *Coriolanus*, Jupiter and the Apparitions (*Cymbeline*), the Musicians (*Romeo and Juliet*), the Duchess of York (*Richard II*), Countess of Auvergne (*Henry VI, Part I*). And what do we know — under his own name, at least — of Sir Christopher Urswick who, in *Richard III*, IV. v, is sent off by Derby to Richmond with a message that 'the Queen hath heartily consented he shall espouse Elizabeth her daughter'?

We may think first of the Duchess of York scenes, detachable from the narrative of the play. The Duchess's part is to listen to her husband as he describes the entry into London of the humiliated Richard, and then to rush to Bolingbroke to beg clemency for her son, Aumerle, who has been plotting against the new King. The scenes, which can be impressive, are too often omitted or scamped. For various reasons it has been found expedient to cut them, as Tree did at His Majesty's in 1903. though no director now could say, as he did then: 'In these days it would be practically impossible to present *Richard II* in its entirety, and in any attempt to stage it, certain excisions and transpositions become necessary.'[13] Tree did not mourn the loss of the Duke of York's set-piece on the entry into London, because he preferred to show this in action, or, rather, as a crowded tableau in the manner of Charles Kean (1857).

Bridges-Adams left out the Duchess of York and the Aumerle scenes from the Stratford production of 1929 which also toured North America. During the winter of the same year Harcourt Williams kept them in at the Old Vic (John Gielgud's first Richard), with Margaret Webster as the Duchess. When the chronicle was revived in 1931 at the newly-opened Sadler's Wells, now with Dorothy Green, it was clear that these were regarded as the passages simplest to cut. A programme note said, briefly: 'The Duchess of York scenes will be omitted at matinees.' Soon afterwards, the Duchess was in when Maurice Evans acted Richard during his celebrated last season in England (Old Vic, 1934–35). James Agate found Mary Newcombe miscast: 'Miss Newcombe, coming to plead for her son Aumerle's pardon, makes skimming entry like a swallow down wind or a seagull lighting on a pier — virtuosity in motion of which any dancer in the Russian Ballet would be proud. Whereat Bolingbroke, who is thirty-three, the gentleman of the period, and solicitous for the old lady, has to say, "Good aunt, stand up!"'[14] At Stratford (1951), though Anthony Quayle allowed us, after the Deposition, to hear some rarely-used lines for that fleeting and seldom-represented personage, the Abbot of Westminster, who invited Carlisle and Aumerle to supper and plotting, we got, until Carlisle's entry at the play's end, no further hint of the conspiracy or of Aumerle's share in it.

The Duchess was out of the Vic revivals of 1956 and 1959. Then in 1964 she was back at Stratford; and she appeared, too, in Richard Cottrell's production in Edinburgh (1969) and London (1969–70).

In 1955, Douglas Seale retained the entire passage for a revival at the Birmingham Repertory[15] where Barry Jackson always insisted, as far as possible, on a complete text. The scenes do act well, though there is one point, the successive rush of son, father, and mother into Bolingbroke's presence, that must nearly always start a laugh from the audience, just as the throwing-down of the gages does in Westminster Hall (IV. i). A director cannot allow the gages to mount up. The text calls for seven throws; towards the end, as noble upon noble joins in, the cumulative effect can be absurd. Anthony Quayle avoided this at Stratford by confining the throws to three, as many as the average audience will accept.

The 'Spy' scene in *Coriolanus*, something that Granville-Barker calls 'a marginal passage of cheerful trading in the ignoble',[16] is IV. iii, set on a highway between Rome and Antium. The characters are a Roman (Nicanor), who is a fifth-columnist, and a Volsce (Adrian), who has been sent out to meet him, and who hears from him the news of the banishment of Coriolanus. It is a good, atmospheric 'bridge' passage; but we have to lose something in *Coriolanus*, which is the fifth longest of the plays. Adrian and Nicanor, like Ventidius and the Duchess of York, have been in and out. We had them under their right names in the Old Vic production of 1938 when Lewis Casson directed Olivier, with Sybil Thorndike as Volumnia, in an ample text (though, curiously, it omitted the glorious greeting to Valeria in V. iii,

> The moon of Rome: chaste as the icicle
> That's curdied by the frost from purest snow,
> And hangs on Dian's temple.)

Adrian and Nicanor were duly on parade at Stratford in 1967.

The Apparitions in *Cymbeline*, though their day is returning, used to be rarer: the sepulchral family gathering of the Leonati that moves about the sleeping Posthumus in gaol. The Leonati talk in rhyme — Granville-Barker, too rudely maybe, has described it as 'jingling twaddle'[17] — before Jupiter descends on his eagle from his 'palace crystalline'. Some critics hold that this is an important theophany. Whatever we feel about it, and it may seem to us that Shakespeare had carefully weighed its effect in the theatre, the Blackfriars, for which he was writing, it is at least worth its place in the dramatic scheme. Harcourt Williams, in an Old Vic programme (the autumn of 1932) explained that his omission of Jupiter and the other ghosts was a 'sacrifice to time'. He found time immediately after this for the Gaoler scene ('O, the charity of a penny cord! It sums up thousands in a trice'). Even Nugent Monck kept the Gaoler in his otherwise ruthlessly-cut *Cymbeline* at Stratford in 1946. During 1951, the eminent Oxford don who played Jupiter in an O.U.D.S. production in the quadrangle of All Souls, arrived, eagle-borne, only at night. Six years later, at Stratford, Peter Hall, allowing the Leonati full play, let Jupiter be heard, not seen; since then the god himself has appeared in full majesty, the right climax to a vision defended by my collaborator on the ground that if the idea of supernatural — providential — guidance is given to the happy ending, then we may be willing to accept what otherwise (certainly in *Cymbeline*) seems over-plotted, or too pat.

Nugent Monck could be a wholesale cutter; he liked to get through a play swiftly and selectively. In *Pericles*, which he did at Stratford in 1947 (Paul Scofield as the Prince), he cut the first act entirely, opening with Pericles cast ashore on the beach at Pentapolis. 'The producer', said the programme, 'is in agreement with the general academic view that the first

act is irrelevant and not the work of William Shakespeare.'
It was not until 1958 that this was performed at Stratford for
the first time during a Festival.

Cymbeline and *Pericles* are not in the familiar repertory; thus
what happens to them is, as a rule, for specialists. These look
anxiously for the brief, bald scene, *Cymbeline*, III. vii, about
the levying of further forces against Britain. Maybe only
specialists are disturbed seriously by the loss of the quibbling
Clown in *Othello* (III. i, and III. iv). For a long period, in
most places, he was an inevitable cut; but Robert Atkins
had him at the Old Vic in 1924, acted by Andrew Leigh;
Harcourt Williams cast for him (1931) so good an actor as
Frank Napier, and made room as well for a First Musician
played by Max Salpeter, then leader of the Old Vic orchestra.
After this the Clown was steadily in Old Vic casts, if not in
Stratford's between 1930 and 1956. The Olivier *Othello*
(National, 1964) did without him. In the previous year, last
of the Old Vic Theatre Company, the director, Caspar
Wrede, restored the Clown as a one-man band, a decoration
quite superfluous.

Contemporary directors can do odd things; but we have
none with the special idiosyncrasies of William Poel, a master
in his own way, who could yet take the heart from a speech, as
Robert Speaight has described:[18] for example, in his London
Troilus and Cressida (1912) he cut from Cressida's speech in
III. ii, 'When water-drops have worn the stones of Troy',
and the three lines that follow. There is now no cutting at all
for the sake of bowdlerization. When Forbes-Robertson put
on *Othello* at the Lyric in 1902, his text emasculated Iago's
part. Further, the word 'whore' was unspeakable: it became
'wanton' or 'one', as in

> I took you for that cunning one at Venice
> That married with Othello.

Frank Benson's company knew this *Othello* scene (IV. ii) as 'the Notta' ('What, not a . . . ?'). Some omissions, merely for the sake of time, were inexplicable. Benson, in *Henry V*, went for many years without the Chorus; and though he restored it for a while at Stratford, it was out again when he took the Bensonians on tour during the early 1920s. The curtain rose, usually to the surprise of many in the audience (for the prefatory talk between Canterbury and Ely had also gone), upon the Presence Chamber and the King's 'Where is my gracious lord of Canterbury?' In our day the Archbishop's long versification of Holinshed, proving that Henry may make his claim to the French throne, has been either heavily clipped or spoken infuriatingly (as in Guthrie's production at the Vic in 1937) as semi-burlesque.

In touring Shakespeare it was customary to omit the entire Induction of *The Taming of the Shrew*, also the scenes in *As You Like It* (II. iii and III. i) in which Duke Frederick, angered by the flight of Rosalind and Celia, orders a search and turns Oliver out of doors. Today these are back, as a matter of course, with 'Hesperia, the princess' gentlewoman', and all. Both in London and on tour, the 'fossil' remnant of the passage for the mock-Germans ('Sir, the Germans desire to have three of your horses') in *The Merry Wives of Windsor* (IV. iii and v) was discarded as incomprehensible; it was left to Terry Hands to restore it neatly in the Stratford production of 1968. Lines always heard now, but cut by Tree for the sake of spectacle, are those before Leonato's monument in *Much Ado About Nothing*, V. iv. There was no need for Don Pedro to say 'Good morrow, masters; put your torches out,' and the rest, for, earlier, Tree had taken much time to show the dawn coming up, mechanical birdsong included.

The murder of Cinna the poet in *Julius Caesar*, III. iii, is one of the scenes that have been brought back. The climax of the act, after which the interval came, used to be Antony's

> Belike they had some notice of the people
> How I had mov'd them. Bring me to Octavius,

though now and then, as at Stratford in 1930, Antony was left silhouetted against the flames of burning Rome at 'Take thou what course thou wilt!' The other poet, the 'jiggling fool' who interrupts Brutus and Cassius in the tent (IV. iii) was formerly a director's natural victim; but he is returning now, as at Stratford, Ontario, in 1955, and he appeared on the Stratford programme of 1957 as Another Poet; in 1963 he was, more particularly, A Mad Poet.

In *Romeo and Juliet* the three Musicians, Simon Catling, Hugh Rebeck, and James Soundpost (IV. v), who have their mild comic relief with Peter just after the discovery of Juliet's presumed death, have now more chances than they used to get. Peter Brook's Stratford revival in 1947 gave them un-expected prominence. *Romeo and Juliet* is a fairly cuttable play but Brook — in a production otherwise containing many felicities — was much criticized in 1947 for assuming that, because most people knew the plot, he could safely do without the Friar's explanatory speech (IV. i) on the working of the potion. In the past, certainly in touring productions, we never had the full final recapitulation of the plot. After Juliet's death the tragedy would be rushed to its end in twenty lines or so.

Even in the least-known plays of all, there are palpable cuts. Thus at Stratford-on-Avon in 1955, Peter Brook, in his justly-celebrated *Titus Andronicus*, omitted from II. iv the lines of Marcus Andronicus with the ravished Lavinia:

> O, had the monster seen those lily-hands
> Tremble, like aspen-leaves, upon a lute . . .

This was cut also at the Old Vic in 1958, but Ronald Eyre restored it in a revival during the Birmingham Repertory's jubilee year, 1963.[19] 'Baked in this pie' (V. iii) during the Thyestean feast at the end, was cut in Birmingham as at Stratford, though we had heard it in a Marlowe Society production at Stratford in 1953. During the preceding scene (V. ii), when Titus, with Chiron and Demetrius, speaks of making 'two pasties of your shameful heads', a Cornish listener may hope that one day the word 'pasty' will be rightly pronounced.

Some of the best known texts appear to be knit so tightly that cutting is hardly possible. Yet Benson frequently played *The Merchant of Venice* without Arragon, though he was included at the Whit-Monday matinee by the Old Bensonians at Stratford in 1932: that afternoon the Arragon just checked a verbal slip in which he would have chosen the leaden casket. One scene in *The Merchant of Venice* has had sustained ill-treatment: III. iv, the talk between Jessica, Launcelot, and Lorenzo, at Belmont, though it was given and approved at Stratford in 1965 and a little of it had been retained in 1956. In the Open Air Theatre production of 1969, Richard Digby Day managed to get the last lines of the scene, beginning at Lorenzo's 'How dost thou like the lord Bassanio's wife?' into the end of III. iv, after Portia and Nerissa have left for Venice. In this Edwardian-dressed production in Regent's Park, Portia was heard to say that her 'Rolls' ('coach') stayed for her at the park gate.

This brings us, briefly, to the matter of transpositions: one that can be complex, for every director treats the text as he will. In *The Merchant of Venice* it was Benson's way to act all the Venetian scenes first, then all those at Belmont; Shakespeare's order was reached only at the Trial scene. Benson used, further, to combine the scenes for Morocco (II. i and II. vi) which need only a small cut to be run on in comfort: a practice often followed, and as recently as the Open Air production (July, 1969). A perfect parallel to the telescoping of the Morocco scenes is the almost habitual running together

3. THE INDIAN BOY

Charles Kean's production of *A Midsummer Night's Dream* at the Princess's Theatre, London, 1856.

4. BARBARA JEFFORD AS ISABELLA

With John Gielgud as Angelo in Peter Brook's production of
Measure for Measure at Stratford-upon-Avon, 1950.

[facing page 49

of the Quickly scenes in *Henry V* (II. i and iii) to the moving
account of Falstaff's death. Because we reach this sooner than
we otherwise would, there is bound to be some dramatic loss.
Many directors' transpositions, as with Benson's, would be
simply for the sake of the designer. Always Benson would
begin *Twelfth Night*, before curtains, with its second scene —
Viola on the Illyrian coast after the shipwreck. The order has
long been familiar. At Stratford in 1947 the first-act scenes
arrived as ii, i, iv, iii; and at the New Theatre (Old Vic
company) in the following year, the night opened with 'What
country, friends, is this?' This order was followed, too, in
1966, when John Harrison directed the comedy at the
Birmingham Repertory Theatre where his work was invariably individual.

Troilus and Cressida which, fifty years ago, was barely known
in performance except when William Poel staged it, has had
alternative endings. When the play first returned to the
regular repertory (Stratford, 1936) — Iden Payne was the
director who included it in a full festival programme — it was
the custom to end on Troilus's lines:

> Strike a free march to Troy! with comfort go:
> Hope of revenge shall hide our inward woe.

Perhaps because of revision, the last scenes are confused. In
both 1960 and 1968 the Stratford productions ended on the
speech where Pandarus, after his curt dismissal by Troilus,
addresses 'as many as be here of Pandar's hall'. Max Adrian
came downstage in 1960, almost a death's head in the darkness; and in 1968 David Waller (Pandarus) and Norman
Rodway (Thersites) were left together with the symbols of
war and lechery.

Inward woe is what many collectors feel when directors
ignore their wishes, and when yet another production passes
without the Duchess of York, Ventidius, Voltimand, or the

4

lines from *Cymbeline* (IV. iii) that so irritated Granville-Barker:[20]

> So please your majesty,
> The Roman legions, all from Gallia drawn,
> Are landed on your coast; with a supply
> Of Roman gentlemen by the senate sent.

CHAPTER THREE

Additions to the Text

The cutting of Shakespeare's text is a delicate and dangerous business. Even in passages which have little bearing on the immediate concerns of the play there may be meaning and purpose. Poel and Granville-Barker were early in teaching this. Poel exposed the inadequacy of the old acting editions. Granville-Barker is at his best in defending some scenes commonly neglected or omitted: Antony and the Servant of Octavius in *Julius Caesar*; Hamlet brought before Claudius to answer for the slaying of Polonius.

A related subject is that of additions to the text. Victorian productions of Shakespeare abounded in tableaux, processions, and scenes without dialogue. They were thought to illustrate and supplement the plays and to be educational in themselves. Charles Kean at the Princess's Theatre, Charles Calvert in Manchester, Augustin Daly, and Beerbohm Tree, all devised them. York's account, interrupted by his grief, of the different ways in which 'proud Bolingbroke' and the unhappy Richard were greeted on their coming to London became at the Princess's a vast pantomimic show using hundreds of supers and, for exciting novelty, a peal of church bells. Calvert's interpolated 'Reception of King Henry the Fifth on Entering London' was again spectacular and again lavish in the numbers employed; inventive, too, in realistic detail, and rewardingly historical. Sometimes these additions imply a sense of deficiency and are to that extent critical.

Tree supplied, by means of a *tableau vivant*, the signing of Magna Charta by King John, an episode wanting, regrettably, in Shakespeare's history.

Daly's *Much Ado About Nothing*, as it was given at the Hollis Street Theatre, Boston, in the spring of 1897, included: 'a view of the conspirator Borachio, under Hero's window, and an apparition of Margaret above, while Claudio and Don Pedro writhed with anguish, and Don John with fiendish joy, in the background'.[1] Daly has not been the only producer to include this scene (it was introduced at the Brattle Theatre, Cambridge, Massachusetts, in 1955 and in productions by Michael Langham, in Stratford, Ontario, in 1958, and Stratford-upon-Avon in 1961) but there is little to be said in its favour. The distancing of the deception through narrating it may quite conceivably have been intentional, and the less we pry into its details the better. The mere fact that Don Pedro was convinced by what he heard and saw should guarantee its credibility.

For some time I could think of only one recent example of a scene's being added to Shakespeare: the burlesque military review thrust with some violence into *All's Well that Ends Well* by Tyrone Guthrie. Other instances came to mind, however, and two or three of them have recurred in a number of productions. Sir Tyrone was not the sole descendant of Charles Kean.

A scene added to *Henry V* is based on, and reinforces passages in the fourth act. After the submission of Pistol's unfortunate Frenchman (in Scene iv), the Boy who has been serving as interpreter remains on the stage. After commenting on Pistol — 'I did never know so full a voice issue from so empty a heart' — and mentioning the fate of Bardolph and Nym, he goes on: 'I must stay with the lackeys, with the luggage of our camp: the French might have a good prey of us, if he knew of it; for there is none to guard it but boys.' Next we have the discomfited French nobles rallying for a further

stand. We hear more of this in Scene vi, after which Fluellen
enters, talking with Gower.

> FLUELLEN. Kill the poys and the luggage! 'Tis expressly
> against the laws of arms; 'tis as arrant a piece of
> knavery, mark you now, as can be offer't; in your
> conscience, now, is it not?
> GOWER. 'Tis certain there's not a boy left alive; and the
> cowardly rascals that ran from the battle ha' done
> this slaughter (IV. vii. 1–7).

Soon after, the King enters with

> I was not angry since I came to France
> Until this instant,

and threatened by new forces of the enemy, he for the second
time orders the killing of his prisoners.

The added scene gives us a glimpse of the Boy's being set
upon by French nobles and cruelly stabbed to death by the
Dauphin. Sometimes Fluellen brings in the limp body, and
the sight of it prompts the King to his outburst of anger.
Sometimes, with less disturbance of the text (Act IV is seldom
given quite as it stands) we have this business alone. In either
case the purpose is clear. Henry's order receives an immediate,
emotional explanation more readily appreciated than that of
military necessity, the danger to the English of being over-
whelmed by numbers. Shakespeare may even have had
something like it in mind (IV. vii. 5–9).

Presumably the added scene is later than the mere bearing
in the body in Fluellen's arms. This I saw first in Glen Byam
Shaw's *Henry V* (with Alec Clunes as the King) at the Old
Vic in 1951. The murderous attack by the Frenchmen I only
saw five years later in an exciting production by Douglas
Seale at Sanders Theatre, Cambridge, Massachusetts. The
Festival Company from Stratford, Ontario, adopted it, that
same summer in Edinburgh, and it has been used more than
once subsequently.

A reader of *The Taming of the Shrew* seeing it for the first time may be surprised by the way it ends. In 1913 Sir John Martin-Harvey found additional lines for Christopher Sly in the old play *The Taming of a Shrew* but did not include the epilogue, in which the tinker is returned to his former state and fancies that what has passed was a happy dream (at least, he remarks, he knows now 'how to tame a shrew' if his wife should anger him). In the autumn of 1931 Harcourt Williams tried this epilogue at the Old Vic, and it was given several times more in productions of the Thirties. *The Times*, reviewing one at Stratford-upon-Avon under B. Iden Payne, 6 August 1935, found the harshness of the story, its brutality even, largely removed if one saw it as 'an entertainment devised for the amusement of a drunken tinker' (who was, by the way, Roy Byford, of happy memory, a fine Falstaff without benefit of stuffing). From this point of view, the epilogue is the necessary completion of a play within a play. Its irony is of a lasting sort, common to tragedy as well as farce:

> The wheel is come full circle; I am here. . . .

Nor can the possibility be quite ruled out that in adding this epilogue we are not restoring to the play something which once belonged to it, something which Shakespeare wrote and then rejected.

In three recent productions at Stratford-upon-Avon (in 1954, 1962, and 1967) and in one at Stratford, Ontario (in 1962), *The Taming of the Shrew* has ended even more elaborately. The players were remembered. Heralded by their trumpet they had arrived opportunely, in the opening scene, to be welcomed and set to work by the Lord. Now, their task finished, they are for the road again, packing up their gear, and with a redistribution of relationships discoverable as Hortensio, it may be, now accompanies Katherine the curst, and Petruchio is paired with Bianca. This is cheerful enough in itself and contributes something to the effect of the play as a whole. Did George Devine think of it in the first instance? Or Nugent Monck, at the Maddermarket in 1951?

One last addition to the text stands apart from the rest through the brilliance of its inventiveness and the appeal which it has possessed for three whole generations of actors. To some of them, I have no doubt, and to a great many theatre-goers, it has seemed an integral part of the play, as Shakespearian as one of its familiar speeches. Irving introduced it in his celebrated production of *The Merchant of Venice* at the Lyceum, 1 November 1879. The scene of Jessica's elopement showed the Jew's house, and beside it a canal and small bridge. After the girl's escape with her lover, a barcarolle was heard, sung from a gondola, and there was a swift passing of gay masqueraders across the stage. The sounds of their laughter and of the music ceased as the curtain descended. It rose again, in response to the expected applause, on the same scene now dimly lit and deserted. In the silence Shylock entered, crossed the bridge, and reached the door of his now empty house. In subsequent performances he sometimes knocked. He did not go in. The distress, the confused passion over his double loss, he expressed only later, when he was with Tubal.

The changes imposed on this added scene by other actors, beginning with Irving's own contemporaries, have rarely been inspired.[2] The reticence of his art gains by comparison. It is noteworthy that the interpolation is still effective in productions which dispense with a pictorial setting altogether, let alone bridges and gondolas — such bumpy gondolas as they usually were! What is more curious, though one associates it with distorted or sentimentalized interpretations of Shylock, it is not incompatible with a very different view of the character. I am recalling in particular a New York performance of 1955, that of James Barbour at the Jan Hus Auditorium in February. His Jew was a proud Venetian merchant, very rich and very evil. In the light of what he was, the return, duly shown, to a house which his daughter found hell, had little pathos. Its appeal to the imagination remained irresistible.

In other words, a reader of *Much Ado About Nothing*, seeing the comedy for the first time, will be unlucky if he finds Margaret (as Hero) dallying with that low fellow Borachio at her window — enough that he hears about it. The reader of *Henry V*, on the other hand, may be shown that very likeable boy who went soldiering with Falstaff's friends brutally slain by the French nobles; and he is even more likely to see him carried in, dead or dying, by a kindly Fluellen. There is a fair chance that this reader's first *Taming of the Shrew* will conclude with Christopher Sly back where he started, and a possibility to be hoped for that the tired actors will reappear afterwards, preparing to resume their journey. As for *The Merchant of Venice*, an increasing number of Shylocks get along without Irving's interpolated scene, but some still include it, to the unconcealed satisfaction of theatrical antiquaries.

Scattered lines and phrases, not written by Shakespeare, still passed as his in old-fashioned performances of the years after the First World War. There were very few, however, by that time. Even Colley Cibber's *Richard III*, deservedly the longest lived of the Restoration alterations and adaptations, had become a curiosity rarely shown. I did indeed see it once: at the Wilbur Theatre, Boston, 18 March 1930. Fritz Leiber, heading what had once been Robert B. Mantell's Company, gave it without mention of Cibber (Richard's notorious scene with Lady Anne, and all) and many in the audience accepted it as Shakespeare's.

Off with his head — So much for Buckingham,

and 'Richard's himself again' were still familiar quotations at that time. Walter Hampden used the former in his *Richard III* in 1934, and Sir Laurence Olivier was not above borrowing both, and more besides, for his film version.

Falstaff, at the moment of his miraculous escape from exposure and shame, still added, occasionally, a phrase just as he springs the trap. 'D'ye think I did not know ye?' he interjected, as he had been doing for a very long time back, before the triumphant 'By the Lord, I knew ye as well as he that made ye'. Allan Wilkie assured me that he was accustomed to use the added words in Australia after the First World War and that he found them helpful. It is my impression — an impression only (alas!) — that I have heard them at least once, not a great while ago.

Again, the proximity of Macbeth's soldiers on his first entrance, implied by the sound of his drum, has been indicated by various means, and in Margaret Webster's production (1941) by an order to halt, repeated, just offstage. But if this was even remotely traditional (Davenant's line,

Command they make a halt upon the heath,

still appears at this point in many 19th-century acting texts) the tradition has now lapsed. It is Macbeth and Banquo who matter — they and the Sisters.[3]

Such small embellishments of the text are still being made and perpetuated, without attracting attention. They are rarely recorded. One, in *Twelfth Night*, proves to be earlier than might have been supposed; a second, in *Romeo and Juliet*, has not yet established itself. No doubt there are still others. Viola's exit, after the completion of her embassy on the Duke's behalf, leaves Olivia unsatisfied. She calls for Malvolio:

> OLIVIA. Methinks I feel this youth's perfections
> With an invisible and subtle stealth
> To creep in at mine eyes. Well, let it be.
> What, ho, Malvolio.
> *Re-enter* Malvolio.
> MALVOLIO. Here, madam, at your service.

OLIVIA. Run after that same peevish messenger,
        The County's man: He left this ring behind him
        (I. v. 280).

Anthony Sharp as Malvolio at Regent's Park in June 1959
repeated Olivia's 'Run' as if startled, speaking it, half-aside,
with a trilled r — and a rising note of interrogation — 'Run?'
This was familiar at the time and, as spoken, was amusingly
in character. Alan Dent in the *News Chronicle*, 9 May 1947,
had scolded the actor Walter Hudd for continuing 'a deplor-
able bit of "business"' which originated, he thought, 'with
the pernickety Malvolio of Mr Wolfit'. And this was 'to
interrupt Olivia with an indignant "Run!" after she has
said to her steward: "Run after that same peevish messenger".'
Conceivably, there was a perceptible difference in the manner
in which the interjection was uttered. The later Malvolio
was more surprised than angry and he was not interrupting
his mistress by what he said, merely thinking aloud.

In *Romeo and Juliet*, Mercutio enjoys referring to Tybalt
as a cat, and teases him with being one. (The cat in the old
Reynard the Fox story had this name.)

MERCUTIO. Tybalt, you rat-catcher, will you walk?
TYBALT. What wouldst thou have with me?
MERCUTIO. Good King of Cats, nothing but one of your
        nine lives; that I mean to make bold withal, and,
        as you shall use me hereafter, dry-beat the rest of
        the eight (III. i. 73).

Is it accident that he speaks of the wound he receives in
the course of their encounter as 'a scratch'? It was a happy
novelty, accordingly, for the Mercutio in Zeffirelli's *Romeo
and Juliet* at the Old Vic in July 1961, to cry, 'Puss! puss!'
derisively, as they fought. Ian Bannen in Peter Hall's production, later in the year, added the same words, but I have not
heard them since. In the Zeffirelli movie, disappointingly,

they were wanting. 'Puss, puss,' might otherwise have been assured of many repetitions in the years to come.

A last group is of added characters — characters, that is, who are unmentioned in early stage directions, and though talked about by others, remain mute themselves. Henry Irving's introduction of Rosaline in his sumptuous *Romeo and Juliet* at the Lyceum in 1882 was noticed at the time. The lines referring to this disdainful beauty had been deleted in earlier acting editions and their restoration was well received. Was it not Rosaline's presence at the Capulets' 'old accustomed feast' which had brought Romeo there? Clement Scott praises the staging of the festivities: 'the gaudy peacocks just removed from the banquet table, the minstrels' gallery crowded with musicians, the sedilia of blue and silver, on which sat the black-haired, pale-faced Rosaline' . . .[4] In what way she figured in the action of the scene, which is complex enough at this point without her presence, is hard to imagine. In any case she seems to have made few appearances after this production.

Rosaline scarcely concerns us; Jane Shore and Kate Keepdown do. As mistress to the King, Jane Shore is repeatedly mentioned by Clarence and Gloucester in the opening scene of *Richard III*. To an Elizabethan audience these references would have carried more meaning than they do to us, since the story of the adultery of Shore's wife, her pride of place, fall from greatness, and pitiful end, was once a very popular one. In *A Mirror for Magistrates* it had been told with success by Thomas Churchyard, standing out through the comparative homeliness of its subject and the readiness of its appeal to emotion. Tom Heywood in his play *The Second Part of Edward IV* was to make the most of these qualities. In *Richard III* Clarence agrees with Gloucester in deploring the influence of women at Edward's court.

> CLARENCE. By heaven, I think there is no man secure
>   But the Queen's kindred, and night-walking heralds

>   That trudge betwixt the King and Mistress Shore.
>   Heard you not what a humble suppliant
>   Lord Hastings was, for her delivery?

It was she, Gloucester answers, who procured him his liberty.

>   I'll tell you what — I think it is our way,
>   If we will keep in favour with the King,
>   To be her men and wear her livery (I. i. 71).

Brackenbury (the Lieutenant of the Tower) here intervenes.
He has already gone beyond his orders in permitting anyone
to talk privately with his prisoner. What they have been
saying, Gloucester protests, is for any ears.

>   We say that Shore's wife hath a pretty foot,
>   A cherry lip, a bonny eye, a passing pleasing tongue;
>   And that the Queen's kindred are made gentlefolks.
>   How say you, sir? Can you deny all this?
>   BRACKENBURY. With this, my lord, myself have nought to
>   do.
>   GLOUCESTER. Nought to do with Mistress Shore! I tell
>   thee, fellow,
>   He that doth naught with her, excepting one,
>   Were best to do it secretly alone.
>   BRACKENBURY. What one, my lord?
>   GLOUCESTER. Her husband, knave.

We hear no more of Jane Shore until after King Edward's
death, when Richard sends Catesby to sound out her new
protector, Hastings, as to his attitude toward the succession:

>   Tell him, Catesby,
>   His ancient knot of dangerous adversaries
>   Tomorrow are let blood at Pomfret Castle;
>   And bid my lord, for joy of this good news,
>   Give Mistress Shore one gentle kiss the more (III. i. 181).

The relations between them are turned to his own account by Richard in the Council Scene. Displaying his withered arm he blames his disfigurement on the practices of

> Edward's wife, that monstrous witch,
> Consorted with that harlot strumpet Shore (III. iv. 69).

Hastings, attempting to answer, is sent to instant death. His execution was deserved, Richard explains to the Mayor in a later scene. So successfully has the traitor concealed his viciousness

> That his apparent open guilt omitted,
> I mean his conversation with Shore's wife —
> He liv'd from all attainder of suspects (III. v. 30).

And the Mayor, in a final reference to Jane Shore, adopts the same moralistic tone.

> I never look'd for better at his hands
> After he once fell in with Mistress Shore.

As a character in *Richard III* Jane Shore was first brought on the stage in John Burrell's production at the New Theatre, in September 1944, where she was seen twice: briefly in the opening scene; and, more effectively, where she is parting from Hastings. *Punch* referred to her as 'decorative but dumb'. With Sir Laurence Olivier again, she figured among the dramatis personae in January 1949, and in his cinema version when Pamela Brown played the part. Later still, Jane Shore was included in Stuart Vaughan's production at the Heckscher Theatre, New York, in 1957; in a fine performance by the Richmond Shakespeare Society in the courtyard of the George Inn, Southwark, 16 July 1966; and at Ludlow Castle in the summer of 1968. At the moment she seems firmly established — never more so than at Stratford in 1970.

Another part for an idle actress (there are so few women's parts in Shakespeare) is Kate Keepdown in *Measure for*

Measure. No whores appear in *Measure for Measure*, any more than they do in *Pericles*, though they are heavily inserted in modern productions of both plays. Kate Keepdown is referred to in three passages — only once by name. Mistress Overdone, brought before Escalus, is charged with being 'a bawd of eleven years continuance'.

> MRS OVERDONE. My lord, this is one Lucio's information against me. Mistress Kate Keepdown was with child by him in the Duke's time; he promis'd her marriage. His child is a year and a quarter old come Philip and Jacob; I have kept it myself; and see how he goes about to abuse me (III. ii. 186).

Lucio himself confesses as much to the disguised Duke, whom he does not recognize. He pretends to be well acquainted with him.

> LUCIO. I was once before him for getting a wench with child.
> DUKE. Did you such a thing?
> LUCIO. Yes, marry, did I; but I was fain to forswear it: they would else have married me to the rotten medlar (IV. iii. 165).

Punishment awaits Lucio, and in his case it is meted out with a certain relish. The Duke is human, after all, and has his own score to settle with this impossible young man.

> DUKE. Proclaim it, Provost, round about the city,
> If any woman wrong'd by this lewd fellow —
> As I have heard him swear himself there's one
> Whom he begot with child, let her appear,
> And he shall marry her. The nuptial finish'd,
> Let him be whipt and hang'd.
> LUCIO. I beseech your Highness, do not marry me to a whore ... (V. i. 506).

On this point, however, the Duke is unrelenting. Lucio is dragged away, protesting that such a marriage is in itself 'pressing to death, whipping, and hanging'.

Our attitude toward the low comedy characters in *Measure for Measure* is very different from what it once was. Their existence is no longer deplored. Pompey is a delight. We even like Lucio (is there, perhaps, a dash of the anti-hero about him?) and do not want him too sternly dealt with. Something to restore the mood of comedy is desirable. The appearance of Kate Keepdown in the person, say, of a strapping young red-head, accomplishes just this. Tyrone Guthrie seems first to have brought her on the stage, 4 December 1933, at the Old Vic, and was followed by Nevill Coghill in 1944. Among later productions in which she has appeared were those at Stratford, Ontario, in 1954; by the Drama Department of Bristol University (Glynne Wickham as Angelo and Elizabeth Shepherd as Isabel) in October 1956; and at the Nottingham Playhouse in September 1965.

Kate Keepdown, when all is said, is of little importance to the plot of *Measure for Measure*, and Jane Shore rather less to that of *Richard III*; whereas the contention over the Indian boy, in *A Midsummer Night's Dream*, affects profoundly not only Oberon and Titania but, through Puck's mistake, Demetrius, Lysander, Hermia, and Helena, and Bully Bottom as well. It is introduced in the talk of a Fairy and Puck at the beginning of the second act. Oberon, Puck declares, is furiously angry with Titania:

> Because that she as her attendant hath
> A lovely boy, stol'n from an Indian king.
> She never had so sweet a changeling;
> And jealous Oberon would have the child
> Knight of his train . . .

The King and Queen meet and as they begin to quarrel Titania explains why the boy is dear to her. Oberon left alone with Puck tells him that Titania must be enchanted.

> And ere I take this charm from off her sight,
> As I can take it with another herb,
> I'll make her render up her page to me.

In the fourth act, after the scene in which Bottom is led away to Titania's bower, Oberon recounts his success. No longer interested in the boy she has yielded him up;

> And now I have the boy, I will undo
> This hateful imperfection of her eyes (IV. i. 59).

The Indian Boy was represented in an elaborately mounted production at Burton's Theatre, New York, 3 February 1854, when the changeling was described as 'never before placed on the stage, though undoubtedly intended to be presented'. He was 'costumed from an ancient print', which sounds a little like Charles Kean.[5] That Kean himself included the character in his production at the Princess's Theatre, two years later, is established by a drawing in the *Illustrated London News*, 6 December 1856. This shows a tiny dark child standing on tiptoe close to Titania, who is confronted by a splendidly helmeted Oberon and fairies of his faction. Meanwhile, in a rival production to Burton's, at the Broadway Theatre, he had entered with Titania in 'a Car drawn with Swans'.[6] In the late 1880s both Daly (very dramatically) and Benson (to hold up a golden veil which floated from Titania's head)[7] made use of him. Later still, he was recognizable at the Adelphi in December 1905; at Regent's Park in 1935 and 1936; at The Haymarket, in January 1945; at Stratford, Connecticut, in 1958; and Stratford, Ontario, in 1968.

Of the 1945 *Midsummer Night's Dream* Professor Coghill writes me: 'I put in *The Little Indian Boy* at the Haymarket. I have almost never seen this done, but he is a tremendous help to Titania to act with during her long speech about him;

5. A WINTRY WINDSOR

Oscar Asche as Falstaff in *The Merry Wives of Windsor* at the Garrick Theatre, London, 1911.

facing page 64]

6. A BAREFOOT AUDREY

Eileen Way in W. Bridges-Adams's production of *As You Like It* at the Memorial Theatre, Stratford-upon-Avon, 1932.

and he can be left howling when she goes off with Bottom Translated.' The speech to which he refers —

His mother was a vot'ress of my order, etc. —

ends with the lines:

But she, being mortal, of that boy did die;
And for her sake I do rear up her boy,
And for her sake I will not part with him.

And Peggy Ashcroft was most memorable just here, in her 'sudden and heart-melting recollection of mortality'.[8]

CHAPTER FOUR

Speaking the Lines

This has to be a very personal chapter. Remembered lines vary in every mind: sometimes because of a reading such as Barry Sullivan's 'The cry is still. They come,' used in John Harrison's *Macbeth* revival (Nottingham, 1952); sometimes sheerly because of the sound of the words, as in Lysander's 'To do observance to a morn of May' (Dennis Arundell; Open Air Theatre, 1936), ''Tis a throne where honour may be crown'd Sole monarch of the universal earth' (Margaretta Scott as Juliet; Open Air Theatre, 1934); 'Nor from the dust of old oblivion rak'd' (Neil Porter as Exeter; Stratford, 1934); sometimes because of a combination of word and gesture, as in Maurice Evans's upward thrust at 'Northumberland, thou ladder Wherewithal the mounting Bolingbroke ascends my throne' (*Richard II*, Old Vic, 1934), or, a few months before his death, Ion Swinley's slow, nobly embracing gesture at Prospero's 'Ye elves of hills, brooks, standing lakes, and groves' (Open Air, 1937). All of these were long ago. They remain printed on the mind, just as surely as Laurence Olivier's famous treatment of the twelfth and thirteenth lines of the fourth *Hamlet* sollioquy (IV. iv) from the Old Vic and Elsinore in 1937: the sudden agonized, spaced emphasis on 'I-do-*not-know* why I should live to say "This-thing's-to-*do*".' James Agate said the line was 'trumpet-moaned':[1] a good description. Olivier, too, returns in the flint-flashed snap of 'The word is *mildly*' (*Coriolanus*; Old Vic, 1938).

66

Still, we have to ask which readings have been generally followed, or which we have heard more than once. Again there must be deviation from the point. Certain test-pieces recur. Will a Hamlet (II. ii) pause to search before he finds the second word in 'This — quintessence of dust'? Will a Macduff make anything in IV. iii of 'one fell swoop', words that came in fire from Shakespeare's pen but that have passed into a cliché? How will a Cressida say 'The error of our eye directs our mind'? (Only one director in recent recollection, John Harrison at the Birmingham Repertory in 1963, has decided that Cressida was not so much a daughter of the game as a Juliet who faltered.)

No scene has been more varied than the interlude of Pyramus and Thisby in the fifth act of *A Midsummer Night's Dream*. This is a comedian's paradise. We can doubt whether the readings in any one director's production have entirely matched those in another man's. Indeed, it might be possible to compose an essay upon the variations: they seem to be endless, and many more performances yet are likely to yield their surprises.

Certain matters in the old touring companies were common form. Thus Snout (Wall) in his first Pyramus and Thisby speech would always try for an odd assonance on 'sinister' and 'whisisper'. Invariably, Wall would forget to hold up his fingers to make the chink, so that the second 'O sweet and lovely wall' was snarled at him, and Bottom (Pyramus) would eventually use a tone of the most profound irony for 'Thanks, courteous wall; Jove shield thee well for this'. Flute (Thisby) would hover, of course, between falsetto and baritone and back again. Starveling (Moonshine), after bearing with discourteous interruption, would dispose of his 'All that I have to say is . . .' in a quick and peevish squeak. (H. O. Nicholson, of the Benson company, was renowed for this part and for his line, 'This lanthorn doth the hornèd me-un present', which a friendly audience was known to speak in chorus.) Thisby, entering at 'This is old Ninny's tomb', would bring from Quince the querulous gag, 'Ninus, man!' And, inevitably, Pyramus and Thisby, at all costs, would bang home their rhymes: 'blood' chiming with 'good', 'pap' with 'hap', 'dumb' with 'tum', and 'word' with 'swerd'.

All of this has been the groundwork. Every fresh director has imposed his own ideas. Thus Quince, as Randle Ayrton acted him at Stratford for Bridges-Adams, used to pause before the repetition of 'bloody' and speak the word in a gulping undertone which made it far more prominent. Tyrone Guthrie, in his Old Vic production of 1951, had a particularly good set of Mechanicals. Paul Rogers, a Devonian as Bottom, employed a mid-Dartmoor accent. (Away from Shakespeare he has been known to speak in the specialized tones of Plymouth.) Guthrie got his Pyramus and Thisby to turn into salutes to Lysander and Helena the lines:

> PYRAMUS: And, like Limander, am I trusty still.
> THISBY: And I like Helen, till the Fates me kill.

Though Helen and Limander are probably errors for Hero and Leander, on that Vic night we preferred Guthrie's gloss.[2] That night, also, the Court party could not resist helping Quince out with the last word of his alliterative marvel. At 'bravely broached his boiling bloody *breast*', there was a chorus that startled Quince, an endearing fusser as Alan Badel acted him. At the end of the play Quince stood, hurt and aloof, until Theseus, remembering that it was time for tact, added to 'It would have been a fine tragedy', a swift 'So it was, truly; and very notably discharg'd'. It was in this revival that Hippolyta (IV. i) recalled that she had 'bay'd the boar', not, as usual, 'bear', with hounds of Sparta.

Earlier in the play, when the Mechanicals first meet, and Flute is cast for Thisby, we can remember how an actor, exclaiming anxiously, 'Let me not play a woman; I have a beard — ', has paused for a second before putting his hand to his chin and adding ' — coming'.[3] Bottom's later 'beard' speech used often to be cut, though generally in these days he is allowed it. One celebrated *Midsummer Night's Dream* reading, often followed since, came when Leslie French played Puck for Harcourt Williams to John Gielgud's Oberon at the Old Vic in 1929. When, in III. ii, Oberon ordered Puck, 'About the wood go swifter than the wind', Puck cried enthusiastically, 'I go, I go . . .', then, as Oberon turned away, paused with a spoilt-child intonation: '*Look how I go!*'

Nick Bottom can use any dialect to please him. We have seen that Rogers used a Devon, Widecombe-in-the-Moor, accent at the Vic. But one has heard Bottom in Scots and in a resolute variety of 'Mummerset' voices. Rustic accents are usually deep in Mummerset. It has seemed a pity sometimes to permit Phebe and Silvius to blur their *As You Like It* speeches with too obvious a dialect. A very difficult part indeed is that of the Clown, the peasant who bears the asp to Cleopatra in *Antony and Cleopatra*, V. ii. Laughter at this stage can be jarring; and usually it comes if the actor of the Clown uses a noticeable rural accent: this, combined with the repetition of 'worm', can set an audience off. George Hayes avoided trouble as well as anybody when, in the disastrous Komisarjevsky production (New, 1936) he spoke in a sustained eerie whisper.

The Gardeners in *Richard II*, III. iv have sometimes used a too determined country accent. Much better was Kenneth Wicksteed's plain, unadorned speech as the First Gardener at Stratford in 1929: the language here is so formal that it would be incongruous to employ the heavily 'earthy' accent one expects from the Gravediggers in *Hamlet*, V. i. In Margaret Webster's American production of *Richard II* (1937) the Gardener entered humming the Gravedigger's song[4] which was clearly intended to introduce him as a comic character. Still, all is well as a rule, so long as the men are not clowned.

Edgar, in *King Lear*, IV. vi, has a problem when he must deal suddenly, on Oswald's arrival, with a burst of Shakespeare's own Mummerset that some young actors have found hard to manage: 'An'chud ha' been zwaggered out of my life, 'twould not ha' been zo long as 'tis by a vortnight'. George Skillan has said that here the accent and vocabulary derive from Somerset dialect, 'an intensification of the one adopted throughout by Edgar'.[5] *The Merry Wives of Windsor* is the play for accents, with the frittered English of Sir Hugh Evans — 'to the Elizabethans', Hugh Hunt has said, 'a Welshman ... was always a figure of fun, far more than a Scotsman or an Irishman'[6] — and the cheerful firework-French excesses of Doctor Caius. At Stratford (1968) the director, Terry Hands, complicated matters still further by letting all his Windsor characters speak with a Berkshire accent: admirable attention to detail, though one doubts whether more than a few people in a given audience have any idea of the sound of Berkshire.

Foreign voices are fairly numerous. Baliol Holloway, who never liked the part,[7] used to employ a fairly thick Spanish accent for Don Adriano de Armado in *Love's Labour's Lost* at Stratford and the Open Air Theatre, but he dropped this for his appearance with the Old Vic company at the New in the autumn of 1949: his last Shakespearian part on any stage. In the same comedy now we are accustomed to hearing mock-Russian accents for the 'frozen Muscovits', the masquing lords. Actors have often to consider what to do with foreign names. Henry V is expected to use homespun (or what we now call Churchillian) French; but how does a King John, in II. i, cope with:

> Then do I give Volquessen, Touraine, Maine,
> Poictiers, and Anjou, these five provinces . . .?

It is the custom today to Anglicize this; but Ernest Milton (New Theatre, 1941) could not resist the most fastidious of French accents.

Pronunciations vary with directors. Fortunately, one has heard no repetitions of the lamentable 'Vee-*oh*-la' from the Stratford *Twelfth Night* of 1943. Cloten, in *Cymbeline*, which for a long time was 'Clow-ten', has now become firmly 'Clotten', on the strength of Guiderius in IV. ii:

> I have sent Cloten's clotpoll down the stream,
> In embassy to his mother . . .

Granville-Barker says of this that, reinforced by several spellings in the Folio, it rhymes, most appropriately, with 'rotten'.[8] Among place-names one of the most arguable is 'Glamis' which in Scotland is pronounced 'Glahms'. Current directors tend to a consistent 'Glam-is', which seems more likely to have been Shakespeare's choice.

One recalls many treatments: Gertrude's 'More matter with less art' as an impatient rebuke to Polonius, who has been wandering on far too long (this was in Ben Greet's provincial production in 1922); the turning of Shylock's lines, I. iii. 105–106, into 'Signor Antonio, many a time — and oft on the Rialto, you have rated me'; Komisarjevsky's hammered insistence in *The Merchant of Venice* (Stratford, 1932) on the rhymes, 'bred', 'head', 'vanished', in the song while 'Bassanio comments on the caskets to himself'; the pun, 'whoremanship' (heard at Stratford in 1951) in the Constable's line, 'You have good judgment in horsemanship' (*Henry V*, III. vii) during the night-scene before Agincourt; Mark Antony's emphasis in the Forum scene (Stratford, 1963) on 'Will *you* give me leave?' in contrast to Brutus's careful earlier parenthesis, 'The speech which Mark Antony (by our permission) is allowed to make'. One has never forgotten the laughter during the Stratford-upon-Avon *Comedy of Errors* (1962), a production, directed by Clifford Williams, that was full of new stresses — especially when Alec McCowen (Antipholus of Syracuse), after listening to thirty-seven lines of fervent blank verse by Adriana, said in bewilderment: 'Plead you to *me*, fair dame?'*

The Benson company had a long-prized tradition that has faded from modern performances of *The Merry Wives of Windsor*. In III. iii Falstaff would come in, singing 'Have I caught thee, my heavenly jewel?' before going on to 'Why, now let me die, for I have lived long enough!' At this point Mistress Ford always pretended to be asleep, for Falstaff was singing the first line of Sir Philip Sidney's lyric, 'Stella sleeping', that begins, 'Have I caught my heav'nly jewel', and goes on:

> Teaching Sleep most fair to be?
> Now will I teach her that she
> When she wakes, is too, too cruel.

In a more important Falstaff scene, *Henry IV, Part I*, II. iv, the tavern play has grown in seriousness after Hal has

---

* Several of the readings mentioned in this paragraph invite annotation. The Queen's snubbing of Polonius is customary and, I cannot help thinking, quite out of character. Gertrude's tact is sufficiently indicated by her correction of the King's invidious

> Thanks Rosencrantz and gentle Guildenstern.

The forced pun on 'whoresmanship' has had a greater vogue than it deserved; whereas the equally strained

> Many a time — and oft on the Rialto,

Henderson's reading, is a collector's item. I heard it twice in 1955, the second time by Earle Grey in the quadrangle of Trinity College, University of Toronto. Komisarjevsky's emphases on the rhymes, not unknown in later productions of *The Merchant of Venice*, is in accordance with the unhappy theory that the song contains a hint to Bassanio to choose the right casket. Let him only continue rhyming and he is quite likely to remember 'lead'. A. C. S.

taken Falstaff's chair as the mock-King. Bridges-Adams, at Stratford, always carried this through lightly. In recent years, performances of Prince Hal have grown chillier and chillier; this has been more noticeable at Stratford than at the Old Vic, though one remembers how, in Douglas Seale's revival (Old Vic, 1955), when Falstaff cried, 'Banish not him thy Harry's company — banish plump Jack, and banish all the world', Robert Hardy's Hal said very quietly and meaningly, 'I do, I *will*'.[9]

Hamlet, which one might expect to be prodigal in new readings, has kept few in performance,[10] though a director is always apt to give us Dover Wilson's version of *Hamlet*, II. ii. 307–310, which appeared in the New Cambridge edition of 1934 and was heard at the Westminster Theatre three years later: 'What a piece of work is a man, how noble in reason, how infinite in faculties, in form and moving, how express and admirable in action, how like an angel in apprehension; how like a god.' Sir John Gielgud, when he directed Richard Burton in New York during 1964, used the more familiar pointing: '. . . In form and moving how express and admirable! in action how like an angel! in apprehension how like a god!'

Some eccentricities, such as Barry Sullivan's 'I know a hawk from a herne — pshaw!', died with their first speaker. Two lines, apparently straightforward, which have been much varied, are I. v. 166–167:

> There are more things in heaven and earth, Horatio,
> Than are dreamt of in your philosophy.

One was accustomed to the snubbing intonation, '*your* philosophy'. John Gielgud chose 'your *philosophy*', but in the New York production of 1964 Burton said: 'Than are *dreamt* of in your philosophy'.[11]

A line elsewhere could have been mentioned with the transpositions: "The words of Mercury are harsh after the songs of Apollo. You that way; we this way', at the end of *Love's Labour's Lost*. Though assigned officially to Armado, in two Stratford productions within twenty years they have been changed. Peter Brook in 1946 gave them to the Princess of France; John Barton in 1965 to Boyet. At the National Theatre in 1968 (Laurence Olivier's production), they reverted to Armado as he came downstage to address the audience. It was in his *Love's Labour's Lost* of 1946 that Brook held for so long — over half a minute — the pause after Mercade had brought to the Princess of France the news of her father's death. In Brook's *Measure for Measure* (Stratford, 1950) the pause before Isabella knelt to beg mercy for Angelo after the Duke's 'He dies for Claudio's death', was timed by one observer at thirty-five seconds. Barbara Jefford was extraordinarily moving[12] here as an Isabella who did not — as most actresses do — make a swift and facile decision, but who seemed to be thinking herself back over the entire course of the play.

Maybe we can end with what has become one of the most watched-for exchanges, from the Church scene of *Much Ado About Nothing*, IV. i. 286–288.

> BENEDICK: Come, bid me do anything for thee.
> BEATRICE: Kill Claudio.
> BENEDICK: Ha! not for the wide world.

It is hard to say why this has been observed so urgently across the years — probably because it is a scene, another of those difficult ones, in which laughter on Benedick's reply can destroy the atmosphere. To play the passage without raising a laugh has become an exercise in technique: the actors are given marks for it almost as if they are riders trying to achieve a 'clear round' in a jumping competition. Through the years much business[13] accumulated about the scene, and various gags, though we never hear these now in any circumstances.

At the end of the scene it became a custom for Beatrice to repeat, 'Benedick, kill Claudio!', and for Benedick to reply, as he left, 'As sure as I'm alive, I will!' Irving and Ellen Terry, at the Lyceum in 1882, had one of their rare disagreements about this, and Ellen Terry, in spite of her distaste for the interpolated line, had to give way.[14]

The habit of blaming the actors for any stray laugh on 'Kill Claudio!' can be unfair, for often the fault is with an audience anxious to seize any chance of laughter. The laugh used to come regularly during Bridges-Adams's Stratford revivals, though in his high patrician treatment of the play — and of the Church scene, in particular — neither he nor his actors gave any unguarded opportunity: certainly not a Benedick of the quality of Wilfrid Walter. It was simply that an audience, because of the early rigours of the Church scene, was ready to be amused, and it regarded Beatrice and Benedick as fair game: unhappily, for Beatrice had to fight to win back the house for her speech, 'Is a'not approved in the height a villain?'

The laugh came when John Gielgud and Peggy Ashcroft played the scene at a Stratford première in 1950. During the following year Gielgud and Diana Wynyard avoided it at the Phoenix in London. We marked then how the passage was lifted gradually to 'Bid me do anything for thee', spoken by a loyal lover; how Beatrice paused for a moment in a charged silence; how the actress held this before she replied 'Kill Claudio!' (words forced from her); and how Benedick's 'Not for the wide world' was quick, low-toned, the almost incredulous exclamation of a man who had not realized how friendship must struggle with love and honour.

The scene has not been done better since in a major production, though Trevor Nunn, as director, and Alan Howard and Janet Suzman as his players, handled it successfully in the Royal Shakespeare revival of 1969 at the Aldwych. In Stratford during the previous autumn the laugh had come.

At the Aldwych, after the early exchanges had been played quickly and fervently, the actors, moving downstage, played the central passage kneeling before the altar. 'Bid me do anything for thee' was spoken very quietly; 'Kill Claudio!' followed swiftly; and there was a long pause before Benedick's reply: too long, no doubt, but it smothered any laughter.

CHAPTER FIVE

Sights and Sounds

In only a few of Shakespeare's plays is a particular season indicated. Falstaff's entertainment in Gloucestershire, in *The Second Part of King Henry IV*, belongs to late summer. Much of *As You Like It* belongs to spring. But although the feast at which Perdita is hostess, in *The Winter's Tale*, comes at a time when the year is growing old,

> Not yet on summer's death nor on the birth
> Of trembling winter,

an earlier season is repeatedly summoned up by the lines; as if spring with its renewal of life were a necessary part of the play's theme. Autolycus on his way to the feast sings, a little surprisingly, of the days 'when daffodils begin to peer'. Perdita is dressed like a spring goddess.

The question of what season to choose for *The Merry Wives of Windsor* has interested producers. Oscar Asche determined on a winter setting and when he gave the play at the Garrick Theatre, early in 1911, the open-air scenes were snow-covered and glittering. Noses were red with the cold, and Falstaff's boy pelted Pistol and Nym with snowballs. Evidence favouring this time of year was discovered in the text. Pistol warns Ford of the fate which threatens him:

> Take heed, have open eyes; for thieves do foot by night.
> Take heed, ere summer comes or cuckoo birds do sing
> (II. i. 110)

77

Hugh Evans, his gown laid aside as he awaits the coming of his fiery adversary, is relieved at length by the appearance of Shallow and Page.

> SHALLOW. What, the sword and the word? Do you study
> them both, Master Parson?
> PAGE. And youthful still, in your doublet and hose, this
> raw rheumatic day? (III. i. 40).

Herne the Hunter, Mrs Page reports, walks nocturnally 'all the winter time', when Falstaff must walk too (IV. iv. 30); and at the play's happiest moment she invites the party to come indoors,

> And laugh this sport o'er by a country fire,
> Sir John and all.

Winter, then, or very early spring. And though one is not called upon to imagine a breaking of ice on the stream into which Falstaff was emptied, his complaints stop only short of this: 'Come, let me pour in some sack to the Thames water; for my belly's as cold as if I had swallow'd snowballs'.

There was criticism of Asche's innovation. Herbert Farjeon, an uncompromising purist, dismissed the case for 'a Christmas-card setting of snow' with the simple declaration that it contradicted 'the spirit of every line in the play'.[1] Yet Glen Byam Shaw, at Stratford in 1955, and Douglas Seale, at the Old Vic the next season, both returned to the prettiness of wintry landscapes and snow-covered roofs. Traces of the idea were still discernible in Falstaff's vast top-coat and Mrs Quickly's muff at Stratford in 1968.

Certainly, much of *As You Like It* belongs to spring. But almost as certainly, it is a play not of one season but of two. The banished Duke on his first appearance calls for a cheerful resistance to

> the icy fang
> And churlish chiding of the winter's wind.

The songs sung by his followers are of cold winds, bitter skies, and rough weather generally. Adam, exhausted, is left exposed to 'the bleak air' (II. vi. 19). It is only later, when Rosalind and Celia are well established in Arden and discover the presence of Orlando there, that we emerge into spring; and later still that two pages sing what Touchstone calls their 'foolish song' of the season beloved of lovers. 'The change is so clearly shown in the play that, once you have seen it, you will wonder however you managed to miss it.'[2]

The real excellence of this idea was blurred for those who first saw it employed in The Theatre Guild's production at the Cort Theatre in 1950. Writing in the *New York Times*, 27 January, Brooks Atkinson referred to Michael Benthall's 'heavy-accented direction' and told of how 'singularly busy' this performance was:

> ... and it is equipped with bird songs, owl hoots, a snow-storm, garlanded processionals, wood smoke, choruses, a fine chamber orchestra; and it is spiced with several episodes of egregious horseplay.

One might add that in its cuts, transpositions, and additions (the concluding lyrics in *Love's Labour's Lost* were both interpolated) the text was remarkably like one of those devised by Augustin Daly near the close of the last century. It was, to borrow Bernard Shaw's word, a *Dalyized* text.

This was not, however, the first occasion on which *As You Like It* had begun with a winter setting, or, more precisely, one of very early spring.[3] That was at Norwich in 1948, when the Young Vic company gave the play on tour and Glen Byam Shaw directed it. Among a number of productions to continue the change of season were two under Mr Shaw at Stratford in 1952 and 1957. Margaret Leighton was Rosalind in the earlier of these, and Peggy Ashcroft, memorably, in 1957. A pool into which Jaques gazed and Martext tumbled was wisely got rid of in this later version which began with a snow-covered landscape and distant castle suggestive of early French miniatures. The advance in season showed in the trees, the leafless branches of winter yielding to the young greens of spring, and there was a beautiful change of lighting. Adam's warm mittens and muffler and the heavy garments of the foresters distinguished the earlier season, and the lighter dresses of the young shepherds and shepherdesses betokened spring.

It is customary nowadays for Audrey to go barefoot. Just when this began I am uncertain. In the early years of the century, for reasons of propriety, persons in classical plays and opera who in real life would have done without shoes still wore curious white stockings on the stage. Miss St Barbe-West, as Audrey, with the Old Vic Company was certainly bare-footed, 16 June 1934, and indeed startled one reviewer of the performance by keeping time, when people were singing, with her toes.[4] But the fashion may have originated earlier, perhaps obscurely with one of Ben Greet's Audreys. It was followed presently by Celia and Phebe, and at last, beginning with Vanessa Redgrave in 1961, by Rosalind disguised as a shepherd boy. Audrey, it should be added, is quite likely to munch an apple. She no longer shows any interest in turnips, her regular fare through most of the 19th century.

Falstaff wears big boots. They are traditional — and the tradition goes far back in time — and has a practical purpose as well. One of our earliest Shakespearian prints, the frontispiece to Francis Kirkman's collection of drolls, *The Wits; or, Sport upon Sport* (1672) shows, among characters from the works of other dramatists, Falstaff and a somewhat masculine but very obsequious Hostess; and Sir John wears a belt, of course, and half-boots with their tops turned down. Half-boots are usual with him thereafter,[5] though thigh-boots (as worn splendidly by Tree) are not infrequent. The *New York Times*, 12 February 1939, describing Maurice

7. DON JOHN IN BLACK

H. B. Irving in *Much Ado About Nothing* at the St James's Theatre,
London, 1898.

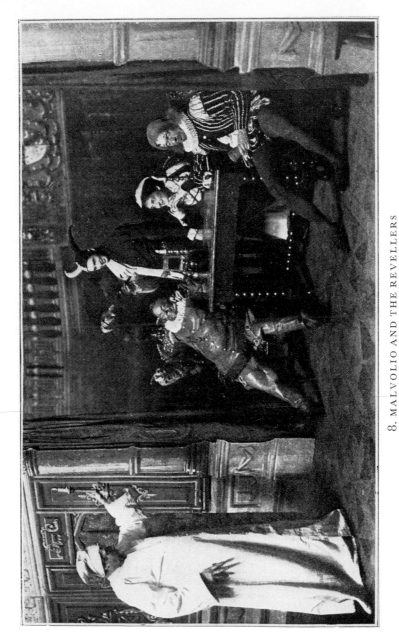

8. MALVOLIO AND THE REVELLERS

Ben Greet's Company in *Twelfth Night*: Greet as Malvolio; B. A. Field as Sir Toby.

Evans's make-up as the knight, assures us that the actor's legs
were encased in

> huge boots, which contain sixty-two feet of leather, as
> against the two-and-a-half feet in the ordinary pair of
> shoes. As an added touch they have been slashed down
> the back, so that they look as though he were bursting
> out of them.

When he plays Falstaff, an actor's own legs must at all costs
be concealed, as absurdly out of keeping with the weight they
now support, and a recourse to padding is not unknown. Ivor
Brown spoke of Ralph Richardson's 'dropsical trunks' in
The Observer 30 September 1945, and James Agate referred
to them in the *Sunday Times* as 'Rowlandson-like legs'.

On the field of battle, Falstaff wears no armour, or at most
a piece or two. It is remarkable how easily this fact is overlooked when we are in the theatre: how readily we accept
the convention once it is pointed out. *Punch* called attention to
it at the time that Richardson (as Falstaff) and Olivier (as
Hotspur) were making stage history in *The First Part of King
Henry IV* at the New Theatre, describing Sir John as 'a
corpulent dotard doing battle amongst a covey of tanks'.[6] But
this discreet warrior differs wholly from those who rage about
him in search of honour, and may as well be distinguished
from them; and there is a practical reason as well, for
Sir John's is notoriously an exhausting rôle, and the actor
has a great deal to do in these scenes and must be nimble. It is
not often that I have seen him stagger off with the dead Percy
on his shoulders, though I have known him accomplish it.

Don John in *Much Ado About Nothing* is likely to wear black
on the stage. Black is well chosen for one born under Saturn,
of a melancholy disposition, and an avowed malcontent. It
identifies him readily as a figure set apart from the rest, an
evil force intruding from without. How early the idea was
accepted I am still at a loss to say. Through much of the 19th

6

century the bastard appeared in a blaze of scarlet and gold. Was H. B. Irving perhaps the innovator? Reviewing a production at the St James's, with Alexander as Benedick and Julia Neilson as Beatrice, the *Daily News*, 17 February 1898, gives a word to 'the grim Mephistophelean Don John' of young Irving, 'whose pale clearly-cut features, piercing eyes, and malicious smile are set off by a black costume'. In 1921, Austin Trevor, at the Old Vic, 'played the villain in black gloves as a burlesque'.[7] Fifteen years later, the writer of an article, 'Costuming the Play', in the *Leamington Spa Courier* (21 August 1936) tells of deciding on gay colours for Don Pedro: 'while in effective contrast the sinister and melancholy figure of his brother is clothed in sombre black and grey'.

Black for the Myrmidons, near the close of *Troilus and Cressida*, is even more suitable, since it accords with the nocturnal imagery of the scene. Hector unarms at the end of a day of fighting. He is taken by surprise. With the coming of night, Achilles tells him, comes death.

> Look Hector, how the sun begins to set;
> How ugly night comes breathing at his heels.
> Even with the vail and dark'ning of the sun,
> To close the day up, Hector's life is done.

The Myrmidons, already prepared for their task, surround and kill him. Achilles returns to the thought of night. 'The dragon wing of night', o'erspreading the earth, now separates the two armies. He orders the body of Hector to be tied to his horse's tail. Black, then, for the Myrmidons will contribute towards making them, as they must be, deadly. Grouped about Hector, and concealing him from us, they become extinguishers of life. Though the stage history of the play is brief, it yet affords a number of examples of their use of this colour, at least four of them from English productions of the 1960s. The earliest is from a Marlowe Society production at the A.D.C. Theatre, Cambridge, in 1922. Mr V. C. Clinton-

Baddeley, who was the Nestor, writes me vividly about the approach of the Myrmidons.

> They rushed — no, crept — in from all directions raising their cloaks like bats' wings and surrounded Hector who was killed invisibly and then they retreated leaving him lying there. I remember Frank Birch [the director] telling them to advance like horrible vampires. I am sure that in 1922 they were black cloaked.

In the case of most of these characters, Don John and Audrey, Falstaff and the Myrmidons, there is small room for disagreement. Falstaff's big boots have become, through the influence of the stage, part of an accepted picture. Audrey is unshod, realistically; Don John wears black by choice and in character. The sable guise of the Myrmidons has a poetic rightness. More questionable is the costuming of two further characters in particular scenes.

Malvolio's interruption of the revels conducted by Sir Toby Belch in *Twelfth Night* occurs in one of these scenes. The contrast between the text and its traditional re-creation on the stage is depressing. From the mere lines one would not have supposed that the Steward was subjected to physical abuse of any sort. Sir Toby and the rest do not, of course, accept his rebuke. They sing at him and may conceivably dance or gambol about him. But there is no hint of their blowing out his candle, if he has a candle, or snitching up his night-shirt, if he is dressed in one. It is he who gives offence, especially in his threats to Maria; and they, and chiefly Maria, who have every right to seek vengeance. In too many productions of *Twelfth Night* the indignities which Malvolio has suffered before his departure leave him the aggrieved party.

But the night-shirt? Like his candle, it has become so much a part of the scene as to be taken for granted in descriptions of it.[8] Often he wears a night-cap as well; or, if not a night-cap, something far worse. A reviewer in the *Shakespeare Pictorial* for June 1936, writing of James Dale's performance at the then Memorial Theatre, refers to 'the fun with the nightcap' as losing 'none of its point by the absence of the usual curling-papers'. Yet in the scene, as we read it, the only hint of the Steward's costume is Sir Toby's uncomplimentary reference to his chain of office: 'Go, sir, rub your chain with crumbs.' Malvolio may quite well have paused to complete his toilet before descending upon those who had 'no respect of place, persons, nor time'.*

As for chronology, Beerbohm Tree was blamed and defended for introducing the night-shirt in 1907. There is a possibility, however, that he may have been anticipated a good while before. For in a promptbook of the performance at the Academy of Music, Brooklyn, 23 April 1864, is the illuminating note referring to this scene: 'Mal. wears long white night gown, white conical cap, leg fleshings and slippers.'⁹

Ophelia's Mad Scene can be played in very different ways and produce very different effects. It is far from simple. The theme of mortality appears in it, and the acute sense of loss, sexuality as well, and gaiety; and upon her return (that

* Malvolio's curl-papers used to be common form in the English provinces, especially during the twenties. Benson used simply to have a fantastic tuft of hair beneath the night-cap. In May 1922 Charles Doran played Malvolio at the Theatre Royal in Plymouth: a very solid personage with more than a suspicion of an Irish accent. It was the fretful-porpentine type of performance that Donald Wolfit elaborated later; Wolfit was in Doran's company. From that night at Plymouth I recall sharply that when Olivia said 'Run', Doran's eyebrows rose, his eyes popped, and he mouthed the word incredulously and silently: I can see now his opening mouth and his expression of dignified horror. At the time it struck me as a perfectly normal joke because in a *Merchant of Venice* (not Doran's) a little earlier, we had had a Balthazar still using the 'foolishness' Matheson Lang had dropped and going out snail-slow on 'all convenient speed'. J. C. T.

ever-surprising re-entrance) the cryptic significances of her distribution of the flowers. What the actress wears in the scene implies how she will interpret it. White muslin is prescribed for her in two acting editions, Oxberry's and Cumberland's, near the beginning of the last century; and white muslin betokens the innocence and gentleness of the character, played always, as she then was, in an expurgated text. Black, recognizable as mourning for her father, came in after 1900.[10] Only much later began the deliberate indecency of dress, the torn gown, or dirty smock, or exposed stays, which accompanies our present-day emphasis on the sexual aspects of her madness. Given this emphasis, the scene becomes one of horror, rather than pathos. It is no longer touching, as it once was. This was true even of such fine performances as those of Simone Valère, with Jean-Louis Barrault at the Ziegfeld Theatre, New York, in December 1952, and Rosemary Harris, with the National Theatre Company at the Old Vic, eleven years later. With gain has come loss. And it is worth observing that what is very like a stage direction in the lines themselves points rather away from current practice:

> Thought and affliction, passion, hell itself,
> She turns to favour and to prettiness.

The casting of certain roles is still governed by habit and experience. In most instances it justifies itself at once. No one seeing *Much Ado About Nothing* for the first time is likely to be surprised or put off by finding Dogberry a fine portly fellow and Verges, for contrast, shrunken and small. Is not the former 'as pretty a piece of flesh as any in Messina'? Or again, in *Henry V*, since Pistol, to pass for what he pretends to be, must be impressive in appearance, he will most happily be exposed and drubbed by a very diminutive Fluellen. Sometimes, however, a familiar piece of casting will be accepted less readily, if at all. Thus, notoriously, Iago, who gives his own age as twenty-eight, may be found matched with a matronly person of whose fidelity it is inconceivable that he should doubt (by merest chance, the Desdemona on such an occasion may not herself be as youthful as she might be). The County Paris is another character who is often treated unfairly on the stage. Shakespeare refused to make him a villain, as a lesser dramatist might have been tempted to do. But although he is not so represented on the stage, his titles and possessions, those 'fair demesnes' of which Capulet speaks so cheerfully, are held against him. Worse still is the Nurse's praise of him as 'a man of wax'. No wonder, then, if he becomes all too often a weakling and something of a fop. That he is called, and deserves to be called, valiant goes for little. Romeo will seem the manlier if he is effeminate. And, another point, when Romeo is darkly Italianate, as perhaps is desirable, then Paris if the right actor is available will certainly be fair.[11]

The importance of such purely theatrical considerations is easily overstated. Elderly Emilias would seem to have gone out of fashion in recent years. One's next Paris, as likely as not, will be as dark as his rival and without a trace of effeminacy. In neither case are we concerned with a fixed tradition. We are a little nearer one when we reach Peter Quince, the much harassed director of 'Pyramus and Thisby' in *A Midsummer Night's Dream*. At any rate, my description of this character as old, or elderly, and inclined to look over the top of his glasses, was accepted immediately by three veteran actors, Robert Atkins, George Skillan, and Allan Wilkie; and Mr Wilkie went on to refer to a member of his own company who had played the part in just this way. Quince, we read in French's Acting Edition (1933) is 'an elderly carpenter, very earnest and industrious. He is not overbearing to the others'. Kenneth Wicksteed, long familiar to Stratford audiences, is spoken of in the *Shakespeare Review* for June 1928 as being 'the frail, timid old enthusiast to the life' — and looks so in a

photograph at the Shakespeare Centre. The same bespec-
tacled Quince appears in a number of pictures, as for instance
those of Arthur Whitby, in Granville-Barker's celebrated
production at the Savoy in 1914, Randle Ayrton at Stratford
in 1937, and Harold Scott with the Oxford Playhouse Company in 1958.[12] For contrast (and even in the playing of this
part there are frequent deviations from the expected), I recall
the desperately intense young director presented by Bertram
Shuttleworth at Stratford in 1949.

The ascription of age and learning to Peter Quince is not
ill-founded. Bottom yields to him in certain matters. The de-
pendent glasses suggest nocturnal study and midnight oil.
Quince knows what the play is about and insists that it be
followed, somehow, despite its difficulties. 'Pyramus and
Thisby, *says the story*, did talk through the chink of a wall.'
A classicist, he is shocked by Flute's gross mispronunciation
of Ninus, and corrects him at once. Flute is no star actor like
Bottom, to be treated with tact and deference. Only that
strange slip of his own, 'he is a very paramour for a sweet
voice', gives us pause. But Quince is much disturbed at the
moment and the substitution of one choice word for another
scarcely deserves Flute's vengeful correction — 'a paramour
is (God bless us) a thing of naught'. Then, too, the part for
which he casts himself ('myself, Thisby's father') is not a
juvenile one. Starveling, who by tradition, once more, is very
aged, and deaf into the bargain, is to be her mother.

Certain properties are associated with Shakespearian
persons and belong to our mental picture of them. Some of
these are conjured up by the lines themselves. Others we have
become so accustomed to, on the stage, that we take their
authenticity for granted. It is hard for me to imagine Malvolio
without his staff of office — the staff from the end of which he
contemptuously drops the ring for Cesario. But although
Shakespeare mentions such ceremonial wands more than
once, it is not in connection with Malvolio; nor for that matter

with Polonius, whom we assume a little impressionistically to be Lord Chamberlain at the Court of Denmark. Petruchio's whip is familiar, too, though he employs it more discriminatingly than he did in the tumultuous days of *Catherine and Petruchio*. Well-known properties in *As You Like It*, unmentioned in the text, are Oliver's riding-crop, with which he threatens Orlando in the opening scene; an absurd bouquet or single flower which William carries, intending to give it to Audrey; and, for Martext, a book, sometimes of immense size and incredibly dusty from want of use (this last refinement was, I believe, Glen Byam Shaw's idea originally). It might be added that even what would seem to be obligatory properties, like the Ghost's truncheon, or Falstaff's, are not always provided in performances today.

The importance of Shakespeare's use of off-stage sounds was brought out, some years ago, in a lively and learned book on the subject by Frances Shirley.[13] References to sounds, she urges, imply with few exceptions their actual simulation. In the Elizabethan playhouses were to be heard not only trumpets, knocking at doors, and alarum bells, but also birdsong and clocks striking, the boom of cannon and the baying of hounds. Lear went out into a storm that was already audible. Macbeth's swiftly formed designs against Macduff were shown to be impossible of execution by a noise of galloping horses. Again, since the references to sounds do not always appear in the form of stage directions, but are found embedded in the text itself, a reader may miss them altogether. Nor are sound effects which may go somewhat beyond the author's intention to be ruled out — so long as they seem appropriate where they occur.

In *Othello*, on the night of Cassio's disgrace, Iago is talking with Roderigo, who at this moment badly needs comfort and encouragement.

> IAGO. Thou knowest we work by wit, and not by witch-
> craft;

> And wit depends on dilatory time.
> Does't not go well, Cassio hath beaten thee,
> And thou by that small hurt hast cashier'd Cassio.
> Though other things grow fair against the sun,
> Yet fruits that blossom first will first be ripe.
> Content thyself awhile. By th'mass, 'tis morning!
> Pleasure and action make the hours seem short.

In the last words he is speaking for himself. Roderigo cannot have found much 'pleasure and action' in that night's doings. But he should, Iago insists. As for what concerns us, his perception that it is morning, we scarcely need to have it explained; which is not to say that explanation does not heighten illusion. I recall that a clock was striking just before, in Margaret Webster's famous production with Paul Robeson; and in several later productions, the earliest, Godfrey Tearle's at Stratford in 1949, one heard what suited better, a distant trumpet call.

Performances of *Hamlet* still begin, now and again, with a clock striking. At Stratford in 1965 when the first scene, so masterly to read, so disappointing as a rule in the theatre, was given its full value, the sound was deliberately exaggerated in volume. Then it succeeded. But so it appears to have done in Sheridan's time. Mr Puff in *The Critic* is demonstrating the excellence of his own tragedy, at the beginning of which two Sentinels were discovered asleep:

> PUFF. Now, what do you think I open with?
> SNEER. Faith, I can't guess —
> PUFF. A clock — hark! [*Clock strikes.*] I open with a clock striking, to beget an awful attention in the audience — it also marks the time . . . (Ed. Rhodes, II, 217).

It is tempting to suppose that he had Shakespeare's tragedy in mind as he spoke. There is little, indeed, to be said against this effect. It is perfectly in keeping with the lines of Francisco and Bernardo:

> 'You come most carefully upon your hour.'
> ''Tis now struck twelve.'

The objection that an hour passes too quickly, if it is again one o' clock when the Ghost appears, is surely prosaic; and there is no need for us to hear the clock on this second occasion. Another sound in this scene I mention only because of its peculiar impressiveness: the sound of the men's footsteps perfectly simulated, as if upon stone. (This was in the production by Alec Guinness at the New Theatre in 1951, a disastrous production, full of interesting ideas.)

Just when it became customary for performances of *Hamlet* to begin with the striking of the hour is uncertain. Another off-stage sound, not unfamiliar in the theatre today, the intermittent tinkling of sheep bells in the pastoral scenes of *As You Like It*, was an innovation of William Charles Macready's in his production of the comedy at Drury Lane, 1 October 1842. Macready had reason to be proud of this, his favourite production, and the sheep bells with their appeal, however limited, to the imagination, were a happy invention and one which has lasted down to our time. The complexity of Shakespeare's pastoral admits criticism, however, as well as delight. There was a sudden baaing of sheep, at Martext's expense, in one Stratford production, and in another the Touchstone (Michael Bates) vented his disgust at life in Arden — he had not yet found Audrey — by himself baaing at sheep who, from the sound of their bells, were only just out of sight.

I first saw *The Winter's Tale* performed at the Boston Repertory Theatre, under Henry Jewett's management, forty years ago. That the Statue Scene could be effective I had been told by old playgoers who still talked of Mary Anderson's performance, but I was struck by the momentousness, the sense of climax and completion, which attended the disclosure of the oracle. This, as a reader, I had not appreciated. Leonates remains infatuated still:

> There is no truth at all i' th' oracle!
> The sessions shall proceed. This is mere falsehood!

> Enter a *Servant*

SERVANT. My lord the King! The King!
LEONTES. What is the business?
SERVANT. O Sir, I shall be hated to report it.
   The Prince your son, with mere conceit and fear
   Of the Queen's speed, is gone.
LEONTES. How? gone?
SERVANT. Is dead.
LEONTES. Apollo's angry, and the heavens themselves
   Do strike at my injustice.

I cannot recall whether thunder came as an answer to the King's impiety. My impression is that it did; and this is borne out by the frequency with which it has been introduced in other productions of the play.[14]

Of these, the earliest, so far as I know, is recorded in Charles Calvert's acting edition, published at Manchester in 1869, which has '*A sudden storm with thunder, &. — great consternation*' begin at the words 'This is mere falsehood'.[15] Is it wholly fanciful to read this stage direction as implying an avoidance of the unheralded thunder-clap, the bolt out of the blue, which could only be interpreted as supernatural; whereas those in the audience who preferred a rational explanation (the shower, coincidentally, happened just then) were here given a way out. Some of them, those who had been brought up on the novels current at the time, would have been well acquainted with such expedients. As for the last words ('Apollo's angry', etc.) they need of course no thunder to explain them, in their full tragic context.

CHAPTER SIX

The People of the Plays

That ardent Shakespearian, the late Guy Boas, in the days of his verse for *Punch*, wrote a poem in which he dreamt that Shakespeare's ghost, sitting at a Civil Service examination, was floored by a question on *King Lear*—

Which Shakespeare answered very badly
Because he hadn't studied Bradley.

Again and again we have wanted the dramatist himself to return for a final word on his characters, though if he did so we should lose the endless fun of speculation, the endless annoyance with directors who go on doing the wrong things.

Take Maria in *Twelfth Night*. She is described as Olivia's gentlewoman; she can 'write very like my lady. . . . On a forgotten matter we can hardly make distinction of our hands'. She will marry Toby, who is her mistress's uncle. Yet over and over she has been represented in the theatre as a pert housemaid. Toby calls her 'my niece's chambermaid', or what the Elizabethans termed a 'chamberer'. Miss Muriel Byrne has warned us not to take that literally. 'It would have been quite obvious from her dress that she was *not* a chamberer, so I can only suppose it was more or less equivalent to calling someone's private secretary "chief cook and bottle washer".'[1] Yet Maria, in the touring companies of the twenties — if not in Benson's — could arrive as a kitchen soubrette; and as late as 1958 there was a similar difficulty. At the Old Vic, early in

April that year, we found that Maria seemed to be 'uncertain of her position in Olivia's house. Was she "gentlewoman" or housemaid? And why the dialect?'[2] Three weeks later there was the same struggle at Stratford: 'Maria's status in Olivia's household is as ambiguous as usual.'[3] In 1966, at the Birmingham Repertory Theatre, John Harrison had Maria, on her first appearance, hanging out the washing.[4] Bridges-Adams, at Stratford, knew her precise place in the household; but down the years one is never sure how she may be treated: often cap and apron are not far away. Few directors have bothered about the implication that the girl must be diminutive: Granville-Barker (1912), deciding that it was probably because the original actor of the part was to be a very small boy, went on to ignore the point.

One would have assumed *Twelfth Night* to be a play as straightforward as any in the canon. Not at all. Who is Fabian, what is he? He is a mysterious personage who arrives in II. v because Sir Toby has invited him to watch the 'sport' against Malvolio. 'You know,' Fabian says, 'he brought me out o' favour with my lady about a bear-baiting here.' Frequently he has been played as a nondescript hanger-on, a gardener, or a cook, one of the characters that haunt the fringes of classical comedy and rarely have people asking questions about them. Because this is Shakespeare, we do ask. Granville-Barker, in the preface to the acting edition of *Twelfth Night* at the Savoy in 1912, when Fabian was that distinguished actor, H. O. Nicholson, thought that he was 'not a young man. . . . He is a family retainer of some sort; from his talk he has to do with horses and dogs'.[5] Hugh Hunt, when he staged the comedy for the re-opening of the Old Vic Theatre in November 1950, decided that he should be played 'as a second clown — a rival to the ageing Feste. Like Feste, he is a member of Olivia's household, but he is younger, less extravagant in his behaviour. If he be a clown, then with reasonable luck he may hope to succeed his rival, for his high

spirits are more strictly under control.'[6] In performance the
ingenuity was complicated: we preferred to think of Feste
and Fabian more simply. As Arthur Colby Sprague has said:*
'The indefiniteness of the rôle all but ceases when we reach
the theatre and Fabian is embodied by a particular actor.
In the theatre his enjoyment of the comic proceedings not
only accompanies but intensifies our own.'

Tyrone Guthrie, in his edition of the play,[7] believes that
Fabian is of slightly inferior social status to Toby and Andrew,
yet considers himself at least as good as Malvolio. 'Perhaps he
is the Coachman or Head Gardener. But he seems too young,
and I doubt whether, in such a position, he would be able to
read. I imagine him the owner of a neighbouring property —
a farmer with plenty of time on his hands.' John Harrison,
at Birmingham, lowered him in the scale: 'Fabian is drying
his hands on his apron: just broken off work. The black-
smith?'[8]

We are wondering now about the other people in this no
longer simple play. There is Sir Andrew. During the early
1920s Andrew was almost invariably a tinnily-squeaking
doll in a starched ruff, though Granville-Barker (1912) had
refused firmly to believe that he was 'a cretinous idiot'. Later
it became the practice to make him neither effeminate nor
foppish but merely a childlike innocent (John Neville; Old
Vic, 1958).[9] Malvolios have varied between a supercilious
young man who had clearly chosen stewardship in preference
to the Foreign Office, but who could move into real pathos
(John Abbott; Old Vic, 1937); a Grey Eminence whose
silences were 'drenched with vinegar and verjuice, and whose
contemptuous eye for Feste was that of a surrealist painter
examining the works of Lord Leighton'[10] (Ernest Thesiger;
Regent's Park, 1944); and a thin-lipped fellow who had

* 'Shakespeare's Unnecessary Characters' in *Shakespeare Survey 20*
(Cambridge, 1967), p. 80.

worked his way up, and 'whose speech suggested his origin by an affected, lisping veneer that flaked away suddenly to reveal the barrow-boy vowels'[11] (Laurence Olivier; Stratford, 1955). To Hugh Hunt, Malvolio is 'an intolerably pompous person, and as such he is exceedingly funny . . . a middle-aged governess of a creature'.[12]

It is a temptation to spend too long on *Twelfth Night*; but important figures need to be pursued: Olivia and Feste. Olivia, in particular, has suffered an extraordinary change. She used to be a stately Countess. In London, earlier in the century, one reason for this was the average age of the leading actresses. It was a more mature theatre world than today's, and Olivia could never have been allotted to the company's *ingénue*. Certainly, in provincial Shakespeare she had always a good deal of personal pomp; and in London, James Agate's notice of Phyllis Neilson-Terry (New Theatre, 1932) spoke for the Olivias of her time and for many previous decades. She brought to 'that wilting bloom, Olivia, all the colour and perfume of a Botanical Garden, with a hint of Queen Elizabeth thrown in'.[13] The 'hint of Queen Elizabeth': that is a key phrase. It is far distant from the Olivia with which Geraldine McEwan, in Peter Hall's Stratford-upon-Avon production (1958) startled her audience. Olivia here was neither the Countess in the grand manner nor the mildly posing romantic that some actresses had made of her. She was without compromise 'a pouting doll, a gawky, giggling coquette, with a voice that squeaks and crackles',[14] and she had no care at all for the verse. Some critics agreed that Olivia had deserved this exposure; and, indeed, she has not since returned to her former state. Today we expect her, if not so resolutely foolish, to be young. Tyrone Guthrie is sure of this. 'Very young', he said in his 1954 edition. Hugh Hunt thought Olivia's secret was 'to balance affectation with attraction, and to underline the gentle but unmistakable comedy of this capricious young woman, who woos so assiduously a girl under the impression that she has found a gallant young gentleman'. Daphne Slater, at Stratford (1947), was enchantingly young but by no means silly; Lesley Brook (Stratford, 1939) was young and 'politely emotional'.[15] As far back as 1923, James Agate, reviewing Viola Tree at the Kingsway Theatre, spoke of his ideal Olivia (which the actress was not) as a 'flamboyantly-bereaved, precious, and ridiculous creature';[16] but directors were slow to take the hint. It is worth recalling that when a boy played Viola, Olivia's infatuation may not have seemed ridiculous at all.

Finally, Feste. Here the stereotype was a tiresome fidget in cap-and-bells who would move to wistfulness with an effort. Just as Olivia has grown young in the theatre, so Feste has been slowly ageing. Granville-Barker (1912) could not think of him as a young man: 'There runs through all he says and does that vein of irony by which we may so often mark one of life's acknowledged failures.' Now he is generally mature. Leo McKern played him for Hugh Hunt as 'a little middle-aged creature' living under a constant threat of dismissal, challenged by his rival, Fabian, and adding fresh poignancy to the last song of the wind and rain: his successor has already been found. Many will think that the Feste Leslie French played so often for Ben Greet and — during the 1930s — for Robert Atkins at the Open Air Theatre, was the most plausible interpretation: alert, swift, seeing all sides of the game, and ending the play, with no special parade, upon the coda of his bitter-sweet song: 'Youth's a stuff will not endure.' One remarkable Feste of our time, never since matched, was that of Robert Eddison for the Old Vic company (New Theatre, 1948), a production by Alec Guinness that 'moved in gaiety and grace, though we marked the latent melancholy of a high summer's day. Feste, realized hauntingly by Robert Eddison, was there to sing of it. The fellow was wise enough to play the fool, and he could match his fooling to his audience; but this Feste — who guessed all the time that Cesario was

Viola — was not a mere twirling bauble of a jester, animated cap-and-bells. He was "long and lank and brown"; his eyes, beneath that comb of greying hair, could search beyond the to-and-fro of summer.'[17] There were earlier 'sad Festes' — one thinks of Marius Goring at the Vic in 1937 — and there have been later ones, Max Adrian's, for example, 'hauntingly astringent',[18] at Stratford in 1960; but Mr Eddison had his own strange distillation of melancholy, and it was not the type of performance that Hugh Hunt was to consider later.

If so apparently direct a comedy as *Twelfth Night* can yield this diversity, it is clear that the rest of the Folio prickles with questions. How long in the theatre has the French King (*Henry V*) been in his dotage? Should Osric be a sinister figure in the background, or simply a fop? How old is Mistress Quickly? Should the lovers of *A Midsummer Night's Dream* be comic? Should Egeus in the same play be comic? The repetition is inevitable, for to aerate parts of a play that they feel, unwisely, should be enlivened, directors have been apt to search too restlessly for a comic approach. And when, somewhere, the approach has been applauded, there must always be imitators to extend the idea.

With few exceptions we need not consider the fringe figures, Lords, Gentlemen, Servants, Messengers, whose purpose is simply functional. But within the last fifty years or so, certain prominent characters have taken on new lives. Thus the lovers in *A Midsummer Night's Dream*, who were straight romantics, are now played, sometimes anxiously, for laughs. In the old touring companies, Hermia and Helena, Lysander and Demetrius, regarded themselves as direct juveniles; they could hardly think so now. Granville-Barker (1914) showed how he felt. Shakespeare delighted in word-music for its own sake:

So recklessly happy in writing such verse does Shakespeare grow that even the quarrel of the four lovers is stayed by a charming speech of Helena's thirty-seven lines

7

long. It is true that at the end of it, Hermia, her author
allowing her to recollect the quarrel, says she is amazed
at these passionate words, but that the passage beginning,
"We Hermia, like two artificial gods," is meant by
Shakespeare to be spoken otherwise than with a meticu-
lous regard to its every beauty is hard to believe. And its
every beauty will hardly shine through throbbing
passion. No, his heart was in these passages of verse, and
so the heart of the play is in them.[19]

Beauty and passion today are secondary; and we may take
up the thread of an earlier chapter and remember how the
intonation of Coral Browne (Old Vic, 1957) suddenly made
sharply ridiculous the line, 'Both warbling of one song — '
(then, with a glow of new and intricate discovery, a sudden
air of surprised recollection) — '*both* in one key'.[20]

As early as December, 1920, a critic was blaming young
Audrey Carten (it was her stage début) in J. B. Fagan's
revival of *A Midsummer Night's Dream* at the Court, for playing
Helena as a comic figure.[21] In 1923 the lovers were still
steadfastly romantic. James Agate, at the Kingsway, said:
'It may be that Lysander and Demetrius, Hermia and Helena,
cannot be humanized. In that case the thing to do is formalize
them, bid the actors ravish eye and ear with gesture and tone.
If these actors have been instructed so, they have disobeyed.
I do not remember ever having known such harsh sound and
ungainly motion as proceeded from this quartet'. One young
actress's voice was 'entirely inapt for poetry'.[22] Then, in the
following year, there came what contemporary jargon calls
the break-through. Basil Dean (1924) directed *A Midsummer
Night's Dream* at Drury Lane, one of the last productions in the
old and waning spectacular style. Here Agate could write:
'The lovers' quartet was of super-excellence. The Hermia of
Miss Athene Seyler was a little Tartar of delicate perceptions,
while Miss Edith Evans gave to Helena five-foot-ten, or

thereabouts, of clucking hen-witted gaby floundering for a shoulder upon which to lay her distracted head. This was a richly comic performance.'[23] By 1937, when Tyrone Guthrie directed the play at the Old Vic, Herbert Farjeon was able to say, as a matter of course, 'With Miss Agnes Lauchlan — the best Helena I have seen — to liven the lovers with her plaintive wit, no one could be unhappy for long — not even those who realized that, the mistakings in the forest at an end, Helena was getting back at Lysander by stealing some of his lines.'[24]

When Bridges-Adams was directing in the Stratford-upon-Avon cinema that served as a temporary Memorial Theatre for six years after the fire of 1926, he refused to let the lovers be throbbingly serious — though he was too good a Shakespearian to allow them to exaggerate the comedy. They were amusingly heightened during the racing-and-chasing at the Open Air Theatre, under Robert Atkins, in the thirties: Helena, in particular, had developed into a recognized show-piece. Earlier, Harcourt Williams (Old Vic, 1929) had been as resolute as usual: 'Martita Hunt's Helena was one of the best things she did at the Old Vic. Her comedy had the brilliance of a Marie Tempest, with just the touch of artificiality that I wanted in the part.'[25] Since then the lovers have been set so surely in the comic mode that we need not add further references, except perhaps to Irene Worth's Helena (Old Vic, 1951), 'a breathless flitter-jill, quacking about with eyes like saucers'.[26] It would be surprising now to see the quartet played, as it used to be: a group of fervent romantics in Greek costume. Hermia's father, Egeus, has emerged as a comedian, though he has taken rather longer about it. From being a small-part angry old man, he has taken on a comic personality of his own, with such a habit as reading from a notebook the list, 'bracelets of hair, rings, gauds, conceits, knacks, trifles, nosegays, sweetmeats,' with which Lysander had won his daughter's heart. But when did all of this begin?

Probably in the middle-fifties, though as far back as 1953 French's acting edition describes Egeus 'as an old man, very fussy and self-important'.

On, for a moment, to the histories. The French King in *Henry V*, his mind wandering, has been familiar through the century's revivals. For many years it was the mode in a Benson production; Nigel Clarke played the part in the accustomed fashion, with its occasional rousings from senility and sudden lapses, when he toured with F.R.B. in 1923. Harcourt Williams, who played the King with Benson at the old Shaftesbury Theatre in 1914, believed the reading to have been Alfred Brydone's; he was in Benson's Lyceum *Henry V* during the spring of 1900. 'Historically', Williams has said, 'Charles the Sixth of France was mentally unhinged, but the character in Shakespeare, except for a certain wildness of phrase, is not mad. However . . . in the light of our modern views on psychology (that queer mixture of sanity and insanity in all of us), to make Charles a little mad requires no violation of the text, and certainly makes it an attractive part to act.'[27] So indeed it was as Williams interpreted it at the Old Vic in 1931, fumbling for a cup-and-ball or playing chess with a boy Fool.

While we are with *Henry V*, how should Chorus be presented? It has varied between Macready's idea in 1839 (John Vandenhoff as Time), and Charles Kean's (Mrs Kean as Clio) twenty years later;[28] the almost too friendly and informal Elizabethan of Roger Livesey (Old Vic, 1950); and John Stride (Old Vic, 1960), at first in modern dress, a jersey and mackintosh: 'On your imaginary forces work.' Sybil Thorndike (Old Vic company, Lyric, Hammersmith, 1928) and Gwen Ffrangcon-Davies (Drury Lane, 1938) played Chorus as male Elizabethans; but later it has been an actor's preserve, with such a speaker as Michael Redgrave (Stratford, 1951) to summon the Muse of Fire. The oddest variant was during a *Henry V* 'in battledress' (Mermaid, 1960): the second part of the night began with Chorus trying to perform 'Roses of Picardy' on a harmonica. Edgar Wreford had the vocal quality, but this was among the curiosities on an occasion — as we might have mentioned in the chapter on cuts and transpositions — when the Pistol-Fluellen scene, the eating of the leek (V. i) was brought forward to the night before Agincourt, and Chorus's first speech was postponed until after the declaration of war.

The Duke of York, Edmund of Langley, in *Richard II*: is he a comic figure? There is no reason why he should be played as one. Obviously he was not a man to leave in charge of the realm; but weakness and vacillation, mixed with genuine courage, are not necessarily comic, as Robert Eddison has shown, though it has always taken a good actor to cope with such lines as 'Come, cousin, I'll dispose of you' in the passage with the Queen (II. ii), or that reiterated 'Give me my boots, I say' when he is rushing off to indict his son before Bolingbroke. William Poel (1899) saw York, defiantly, as comic. Treatment has long fluctuated. Frank Napier's testiness roused laughter in the 1934 production at the Old Vic (Maurice Evans as Richard); and in 1937 Herbert Farjeon, reviewing Gielgud's revival at the Queen's, remarked upon 'the humorous old Duke of York of Mr George Howe, to whose admirable discretion one would safely entrust all the dullest barons and bishops in Shakespeare'.[29] Gielgud himself has written:

'York, used by Shakespeare as a kind of wavering chorus throughout the play, touching yet sometimes absurd, can be of great value, provided that the actor and director can contrive between them a tactful compromise between comedy and dramatic effect. To make him a purely farcical character (as has sometimes been attempted) weakens the play, and is quite opposed, it seems to me, to the intention of the dramatist.'[30]

Granville-Barker, in a letter to Gielgud during 1937, suggested that the Duke was 'rather a Polonius — a first study for him?'[31] Michael Gwynn's Duke, nervous and teasy at Stratford (1951), took a hint from the phrase, 'prisoner to the palsy': except in such a speech as the narrative of the return to London, he was often comically fretful, though sensitive enough to keep on the right side of the border.

Often stage performance can illuminate something that may be overlooked in the study. Several watchers of consecutive productions of *Richard II* and *Henry IV, Part I* had never realized before 1951, with so much clarity, that 'young Harry Percy', with forty-four lines in *Richard II*, was the Hotspur of the succeeding play. This should be obvious; but until 1951 at Stratford one had usually seen Harry Percy acted as any personable juvenile, with nothing to show in him the Hotspur-to-be, 'the light by which the chivalry of England moved'. Gordon Crosse, experienced critic without professional portfolio, recognized the quality in Frank Duncan, who played Hotspur for the Old Vic company at the New in 1947: 'By his vigorous, youthful enthusiasm, he showed us Hotspur in embryo.'[32] At Stratford this was made apparent when Robert Hardy, in Anthony Quayle's production of *Richard II*, gave to Percy a thick, Border-Northumbrian accent which was used later by Michael Redgrave in his Hotspur (Quayle and John Kidd directed *Henry IV, Part I*). The accent was the season's solution of Lady Percy's line in *Part II*, 'Speaking thick, which nature made his blemish.' Most commentators agree that 'thick' is used in the sense of 'thick and fast', but through the years a convention has risen that Hotspur stammered — as, for example, Matheson Lang did (His Majesty's, 1914; he was the English innovator, at Tree's suggestion), Baliol Holloway at Stratford in 1923, and Gyles Isham, also at Stratford, in 1931. The stammer was taken to its fullest theatrical effect by Laurence Olivier (Old Vic company, 1945), when, electing to halt throughout on the

letter 'w', he died in combat with the last word still struggling for
utterance.[33] Nothing could have pointed the text more surely:

> No Percy, thou art dust
> And food for —— (*Dies*)
> PRINCE HENRY: For worms, brave Percy; fare thee well,
> great heart.

Olivier's technique gratified stammerers who have often
known their complaint to be monstrously abused in performance. No stammerer is vague; he has his own close pattern
of difficult sounds (a hard 'd', for instance); and it has been
absurd to listen to some actors — conventionally the Tailor
in *The Taming of the Shrew* is a stammerer — who have merely
fizzed and bubbled at random. John Neville had the true
method at the Old Vic (1955): his Hotspur chose, accurately
and consistently, to stammer on the 'm' sound.[34]

One more figure from the histories: Mistress Quickly,
hostess of the Boar's Head. She has generally been shown as
an aged dame, tiresomely sometimes, for little can be more
conventional than the stage performance of a raucous
character-woman. Then, in the spring of 1960, Bernard
Hepton, who directed the two parts of *Henry IV* at the
Birmingham Repertory — the first of them in a text that
Barry Jackson had arranged earlier — allowed Elizabeth
Spriggs to present the Quickly of her imagination. Though
she had neither read nor seen the part previously, she thought
herself into it with so much honesty and confidence as a fresh,
flexibly-spoken woman in her thirties, voluble, wide-eyed, and
gullible, that it would be hard to face again some wheezing
ancient of the rustier mirth.[35]

Forward to the tragedies: to *Hamlet* and to a sinister Osric.
Here, again, is a character that has grown from a 'water-fly',
a fop round the court, to a watchful minion of the King, a
collaborator in evil. Professor Dover Wilson assumed from
the lines in V. ii, those of Laertes,

As a woodcock to mine own springe, Osric!
I am justly killed with mine own treachery,

that Osric was an accomplice in the plot and knew the secret
of the unbated and poisoned sword.[36] As presented in Hugh
Hunt's revival (New, 1950), Osric was 'a sly, saturnine figure,
a sinister and dangerous accomplice of the King'.[37] Hunt
described him as 'the typical courtier of the age — the syco-
phant, the clever swordsman, the time-server, the flatterer
whom Shakespeare most disliked and most ridiculed . . .
It is a telling part, this messenger of death caparisoned in
finery and a master of courtesies.'[38] Indeed; but it would have
astonished Osrics of the older school, who were simply popin-
jays about the court. For example, 'The Osric of Mr Martin
Harvey was just what it should be, perky, affected, and
inoffensive'[39] (Forbes-Robertson's production, 1897). Twelve
years before this, Clement Scott had said of the same actor,
with Irving at the Lyceum: 'Mr Martin Harvey gave a
reading of the part that may be highly commended. Osric,
with his pleasant voice and refined manner, was affected
and silly, without ceasing to be a courtier.'[40] On tour during
the twenties, Osric was uncomplicated comic relief, no more.
When John Barrymore brought his Hamlet to London (1925),
the English actor, Frederick Cooper, was 'a charming little
fop who did not seem, for once, bent on making the most of
slight but flashy opportunities'.[41] Soon after this, Osric
would grow slowly more dangerous; by now he is the King's
demi-devil. Were he really so, then his escape from punishment at the close of the play would be unparalleled in
Shakespearian tragedy.

Lastly, three characters, all from the comedies: Gonzalo,
Sir Eglamour, Balthazar. Gonzalo, the 'honest old counsellor'
of *The Tempest*, has generally been easier in the text ('I would
with such perfection govern, sir, T'excel the golden age') than
he has been on the stage where elderly sententiousness can

be tiring in representation. To get over this, directors have
made an occasional, but ephemeral, attempt to turn the part
towards comedy; but the last word must be with convention,
as in the straightforward performance at Chichester Festival
during 1968. We meet *The Two Gentlemen of Verona* so relatively
seldom that not much has been said about Sir Eglamour,
'agent for Silvia in her escape', as he has been described. It is
the custom now, as at the Old Vic (1957) and at the Open
Air Theatre (1968 and 1969) to present this romantic figure
as a kind of gently-caricatured Quixote, though there is little
justification in a text that calls Eglamour 'valiant, wise,
resourceful, well-accomplished', and speaks of his vow of
chastity since his true love died.

As for Balthazar in *The Merchant of Venice*, 'a youth full of
enthusiasm', said Ben Greet in 1913, he has one of the Folio's
most theatrically pleasant single-line parts, though it is
extended if he is also the Messenger or Servant in II. ix who
brings, in terms amusingly inflated, the news of Bassanio's
arrival. But Balthazar depends on the line in III. iv when,
after Portia has bidden him haste to Padua, to bear a letter to
Bellario, and to return 'with imagin'd speed', to the Venetian
ferry, he replies with dignity, 'Madam, I go with all convenient
speed'. In every touring company, Benson's, Baynton's,
Doran's, and the rest, the line was treated as James Agate
describes it in a review of Stanley Bell's old-style London
production at the Alhambra in 1934. This was almost the last
'realistic' West End Shakespeare, with a load of representa-
tional scenery. Balthazar on that occasion was John Sullivan.
'He has a terrific success with his single line', wrote Agate.
'On the night I attended, the line was delivered with such
solemnity and grandeur that the house rose at Mr Sullivan.'[42]
Possibly the place for this might be under textual readings;
but the speaking of a single line does flash up an entire
character. Hugh Hunt (Old Vic, 1953), accepting Balthazar
as the early messenger or Servant — and today the parts are

generally fused — wanted him played with 'something of the mannered courtesy which will warrant Portia's remark to him, "What would my lord?"'[43] Balthazar in his second scene reminds us of a minor Malvolio, for Malvolio, as we have observed in an earlier chapter, had the same reaction when told to 'run after that same peevish messenger, the county's man'. It is among the jokes that wear very well after 370 years.

CHAPTER SEVEN

Stages and Staging

Young playgoers, bred to the rebellious variety of modern Shakespeare staging, its freedom broadening from experiment to experiment, find it hard to imagine what has gone before. Indeed, they wonder if there could ever have been a primeval world of the theatre, a world of illusion before Brecht, a world of Shakespeare before the Royal Shakespeare Company, a world where a distinguished writer could say in 1944: 'The art of stage production and design in this country has on the whole pursued a course of modesty and sobriety; the major eccentricities of theatrical theory seem to have passed it by.'[1]

In one sense the stage today is no longer a mystery. More often than not a playgoer at Stratford-upon-Avon finds that the curtain is up, with the stage set; in at least one recent production (*Twelfth Night*, 1969) Orsino had already taken his place. The set is likely to be permanent, though this has to mean now and then — as in the Stratford *Pericles* and *Winter's Tale* of 1969 — a strong call on the audience's imagination. By now most audiences are obediently house-trained. What might really astonish them would be a return to the methods of Beerbohm Tree, or of English provincial companies that held to an old mode years after Tree's death, if with none of his resources. Thus, in so apparently direct a play as *The Merchant of Venice*, Henry Baynton — touring in the early 1920s — would lower his curtain thirteen times between

108 SHAKESPEARE'S PLAYS TODAY

scenes. (Fortunately there were no calls at the end of every
act, something that would continue in London until the mid-
twenties). In America, Fritz Leiber, at the Wilbur Theatre,
Boston (1930) had five intervals in his *Richard III*: he was
staging a six-act Cibber version.[2] At this point one thinks
of Sheridan's Mr Puff on another occasion: 'As we have the
scenes and the dresses, egad, we'll go to't as if it were the first
night's performance — but you need not mind stopping
between the acts.'

Tree's opulence (his immense *Twelfth Night* garden, in a
Punch-coined word, was 'swardy') and his gleaming Alma-
Tadema marbles would be regarded now as horrific extravagances,[3] even though audiences still like 'something to look at':
the tag is lasting. These effects enraptured playgoers of a period
whose taste in the detail of classical production was not ours.
Certainly we would hardly say of an Oberon, as the *Pall Mall
Gazette*[4] did of Julia Neilson: 'For her singing no praise can be
too high. There is a rich thrill in her tones that suggests some
gorgeous Eastern bird.' Gorgeous was the adjective at that
plumaged period. Only such a resolute innovator as William
Poel, working — more or less exempt from public haunt — in
his return to the conditions of the Elizabethan stage as he
imagined them, could afford to be austere (and Poel's austerity
could be capricious). Shakespeare had to be decorated,
though before long, Gordon Craig would use his own forms
of stringent simplification: designs uninhibited by regard for
theatre mechanics. Like Granville-Barker, whose Savoy
revivals (1912–14) wrecked the worst conventions of Shakespeare performance, Craig would be a lasting influence[5]
in years ahead. Stages were progressively uncluttered;
grandiose sets vanished. It could seem odd when in the spring
of 1934, at the Alhambra, London, Godfrey Tearle's Mark
Antony (*Julius Caesar*) appeared among tons of marble, and
The Merchant of Venice had its shaky gondolas beneath the
Rialto bridge and its twittering birds in an umbrageous

Belmont. These were London's last West End productions that derived in spirit from Tree. Wholesale realistic staging was left to the cinema, a tradition exemplified in the glossy futilities of Reinhardt's *Midsummer Night's Dream* film (1935).

Regular visitors to Stratford-upon-Avon, from the opening of the new Shakespeare Memorial Theatre in 1932, will have observed every spoke in the twisting wheel of fashion. The fastidious W. Bridges-Adams, student of Poel and Granville-Barker though he was, could not resist just five minutes with the old spectacular method: he began his masque treatment of *The Tempest* (1934) with a startling picture of a full-rigged galleon struggling in the trough of the waves, something unmatched on this stage before or since. B. Iden Payne, during his directorship, (1935–42) returned steadily to an Elizabethan-compromise method that would become a little monotonous: the use of a false proscenium, a penthouse roof supported by two pillars between which Elizabethan pages drew curtains when only the forestage was needed, and opened them for a new inner setting on an upper or lower level.

Against this economical plan were the flamboyances of Theodore Komisarjevsky. Though he could insist on as swift a pace as anyone, he had his idiosyncratic ideas of décor: the scrolled aluminium screens of *Macbeth* (1933), for example, or the great flight of stairs in *King Lear* (1936). After the war, Stratford would move from the romantic Watteau designs for Peter Brook's revival of *Love's Labour's Lost* in 1946 and the most floriferous decoration of Michael Benthall's *A Midsummer Night's Dream* in 1949, to what appeared then to be the ultimate austerity, Michael Langham's production of *Hamlet* in 1956. The stage was bare except for an isolated arras that stood like a furled tent against a dead-black background. Lighting alone built the scenes from the darkness. 'Claudius,' wrote a critic,[6] 'says at the end, "Set me the stoups of wine there beside me." At Stratford he cannot say "upon the table" because there is no table. The mind swings instinctively to

Alice, "There were no birds to fly."' Held at the time to be the
last word in severity, it might have been taken for granted at
Stratford during the late sixties where generally the stage was
flat, steps had practically disappeared, and audiences hardly
noticed the change. One writer did. The actor-critic, Robert
Speaight, said admirably in *Shakespeare Quarterly* (Autumn
1965): 'I am amused by the whirligig of scenic fashions at
Stratford. Ever since Mr Hall happily abolished his staircase
in the *Dream*, platforms have been taboo and steps only grudg-
ingly admitted. Every opportunity is given for the actors to sit
on the ground, and every opportunity is taken. One doesn't
necessarily complain, but an occasional declivity can be useful.'

One of the last more elaborate productions was also one of
the slowest, the *Othello* of 1961. Few of the old actor-managers
would have found Franco Zeffirelli's sets alarmingly ornate,
yet they took so long to change that the production appeared
to be moving at an 'Early Decorated' pace, a dulling of device
by coldness and delay. For all his theatrical qualities, Zeffirelli
is a fussy director. Though his Old Vic *Romeo and Juliet* (1960)
was in the right latitude, beneath the sun-scorched walls of a
credible Verona, the treatment was far too busy and unselec-
tive; Zeffirelli had considered the play like an ardent Italian
who could not hear English verse, and his cuts were so ill-
judged that, for example, the Mantua scene (V. i) opened at
'Then I defy you, stars'.[7]

Through all the misty battles of theory and practice one
fact has shone: audiences do want to see something, even if
nobody asks any longer for the ponderous illusions of Tree
and his reconstruction of Cleopatra's barge upon the Cydnus.[8]
Today this visual pleasure must come principally from the
costumes, often from a director's trick of switching a play to
any decorative period and hunting for a relevant excuse —
frequently with anxious programme notes (there should be an
anthology of these miscellaneous writings) and frequently
without any excuse whatever. One remembers Michael

Benthall's resolve (Stratford, 1948) to put *Hamlet* into early-Victorian costume and a Winterhalter-Waterhouse Elsinore of fretted arcades; Isamu Noguchi's designs for *King Lear* (London, 1955), with its space-men suits, inverted-hatstand crown, dispersed geometrical shapes, and chairs like bulbous boomerangs; and the charm of Douglas Seale's decision (Stratford, 1958) to see *Much Ado About Nothing* through the eyes of Tissot (roughly 1851). Zeffirelli went much too far when in 1965 he staged the same patrician comedy at the National Theatre, London, as a late 19th-century bourgeois Sicilian romp.[9] In a 'Pop Theatre' *Midsummer Night's Dream* at Edinburgh Festival in 1967, Bottom — as Frank Dunlop directed him — wore among other things a leather-studded jacket and a crash helmet, and Quince appeared first in a drooping moustache, a bowler hat, steel-rimmed spectacles — traditionally, his sight troubled him — a complex of waistcoat-and-cardigan, and a khaki office overall. Tyrone Guthrie, in his expert fantastications, has always had an eye for costume: thus, in *Troilus and Cressida* (Old Vic, 1956), Ulysses became — properly, no doubt — an Admiral, and Ajax a puffily scarlet General, period 1913; the frivolous Trojans were resplendent in yellow, like musical-comedy dragoons, with plumed brass helmets and breastplates that flickered like heliographs across the theatre; and the factious Greeks, in spiked helmets and bristly moustaches, were given where possible to Germanic jack-booted clanking and heel-clicking.

One major reason for changes in the century's staging has been the desire for continuous performance. Critics, even remembering Granville-Barker a few years before, were amazed at the speed of Bridges-Adams's revival of *Henry V* (London, 1920) by the Stratford company. Archibald Haddon, quoting Chorus, 'Thus with imagined wing our swift scene flies', noted[10] that the uncut play took less than three hours: nineteen scenes with a single short interval. 'Except for a few full-stage sets the episodes were presented in panel form between sliding curtains. The play, to modern eyes, is essentially a spectacular work and therefore none too amenable to such treatment; yet the total effect was pictorial. . . . Shakespeare can be adapted to contemporary conditions of time and temper without sacrifice of artistry.' Today intervals are cut to a single break, or, at the most, two;[11] and, more and more, scenes, in their rapid progress, are juxtaposed or imaginatively overlapped. Frank Hauser did this excitingly in his Oxford Playhouse *Antony and Cleopatra* (1965) when, for example, the often-cut Syrian scene (III. i) for Ventidius, Silius, and the Roman army ('Now, darting Parthia, art thou struck') was set immediately against the revellers on Pompey's galley (II. vii). One can recall also Cleopatra still visible as the first Roman scene (I. iv) began in Michael Langham's production of *Antony and Cleopatra* at Stratford, Ontario, in 1967; and there was an uncommonly swift and forcible *Henry V* by the Ontario company at the Assembly Hall, Edinburgh, in 1956, a revival insufficiently praised for its cohesion and technical address. From Bridges-Adams's superb Stratford-upon-Avon production of *Richard II* (1929; acted in Boston, Massachusetts in 1930) comes another type of overlapping: the moment when the laughter of the King and his favourites outside Gaunt's sick-room mingled with the last lines of the 'England' speech.[12]

It was the wish for speed that finally established the permanent set, devised craftily in all manner of forms, awkward sometimes in maintaining its first localizations, but relying upon the audience's readiness to think itself into the scene — like Ivor Brown's Master Sanguine, to believe what it is told. As a prologue-writer has said[13] of sights upon the out-thrust prow of the Elizabethan platform stage:

Egypt and Arden, Athens, Elsinore,
Wind on the heath or wreck upon the shore,

The morning's glimmer and a midnight's dread
('In the same figure like the king that's dead'):
All this is captured in the verse that brings
To questing life the captains and their kings,
Their castles, taverns, banners, blazonry,
The temple-haunting martlet's mansionry . . .

Playgoers, over a gap of centuries, have recovered the old flexible imagination. After all, Shakespeare was not in any doubt when Chorus explained that the cockpit of the Globe held the vasty fields of France.

Choice from scores of permanent sets is a problem. One can remember, maybe, the cunningly theatrical structure, rostrum upon rostrum, that Tyrone Guthrie employed for the Olivier *Hamlet* at the Old Vic in the spring of 1937 and later in the Kronborg courtyard at Elsinore; Tanya Moisiewitsch's staging, spaciously conceived and of sweeping dignity, for Guthrie's Stratford-upon-Avon *Henry VIII* of 1949 (Guthrie used upon it the steady truth of almost uncoloured lighting);[14] and Hutchinson Scott's mistily shining set of filigreed pillars, with a small balcony at the side, for the Bristol Old Vic's *Two Gentlemen of Verona* (directed by Denis Carey; Old Vic, London, 1952).[15] The briefest thought will recreate set upon set: Leslie Hurry's for *The Tempest* (Old Vic, 1962), a rocky sea-shore against a sky apparently of veined marble; the unfortunate Stratford *Tempest* of 1963 when the island was environed by a translucent shell or skin, and the wrecked courtiers were brought in upon a travelling belt; and an *As You Like It* (National, London, 1967) with an all-male cast, that was played in an Arden of tubular Perspex trees, backed by what resembled crumpled and tattered mock-lace mats, flicking up and down as needed. For her exasperating *Henry IV*, a conflation of both parts, at the Assembly Hall, Edinburgh in 1964 (Quatercentenary year, no less) Joan Littlewood 'stretched across the hall, from side to side, a kind of dyke, a high oblong stage that divided the audience into halves'.[16] Upon this her company had to manoeuvre, with much restlessness and showing of backs, so that each half of the auditorium could get a share of what was going on. It went on in costumes that included a curly-brimmed topper, jeans, and carpet slippers.

Peter Brook's production of *King Lear*, with its tall, coarse-textured off-white screens, its thunder-sheets, and its bare, flat stage, was to become internationally famous. One of the oddest permanent sets on record was that designed by Lila de Nobili for the Stratford-upon-Avon *Cymbeline* in 1957. Peter Hall, wishing to meet a fairy-tale on its own terms, sanctioned something that ·— like the first theatrical presentation of *Under Milk Wood* — tried to put everything upon the stage at once, breaking the rule that a permanent set should never let us know it is there. That night the Stratford stage lay between great oaks, cast from Stratford trees, and before a cluster of isolated features that included a grotto, a Renaissance interior, a church tower, stairs that curled enticingly in various cracks, and the pillars of a ruined abbey in front of which Imogen went to bed.

More successful, and sharply memorable, was Leslie Hurry's design for the Stratford-upon-Avon *Troilus and Cressida* of 1960 (and Edinburgh Festival, 1962). The plains of Troy were represented by a symbolic cockpit, a shallow, octagonal platform, thickly strewn with white sand and set before an abstract backcloth the hue of dried blood. Here love and chivalry were grated to dusty nothing. 'As false as sandy earth', says Cressida, and in those surroundings the phrase had an uncommon sting.

There have been various efforts, mixed in their effect, to make one architectural structure, functional, harmonious, and unlocalized, serve for a sequence of plays. Thus one recalls how Tyrone Guthrie, in the Old Vic–Sadler's Wells season of 1933–34, employed an abstract design by an architect, Wells Coates, that proved in practice to be as obtrusive as it was contemporary. Though it was distinctly handsome, said Guthrie, 'whatever colour it was painted, however it was lit, it appeared not as a merely functional background to the play but also as a powerful, stridently irrelevant competitor for the audience's attention'.[17] Tanya Moiseiwitsch devised most serviceably a roughly oak-timbered, bannered set for the Stratford historical tetralogy of 1951, on one side a throne, on the other a penthouse; and Douglas Seale employed Finlay James's severely beautiful Gothic triptych setting for the trilogy of *Henry VI*, staged at Birmingham Repertory through the faith of Sir Barry Jackson and brought to the Old Vic, London, in the summer of 1953. The Old Vic company, a few weeks after this, began its season with a three-arched screen, Palladian in style, that was intended to serve for the entire Five-Year Plan (the staging of the complete Folio); it vanished fairly soon. Stratford-upon-Avon, for several productions in 1969, used variations upon an uncompromising design by Christopher Morley that irresistibly reminded one critic of a vast, high bath-room.

Anxiously, directors have sought for a closer, more Eliza-bethan intimacy between stage and audience, something hard to achieve in those vast Victorian theatres when it could seem to be a day's march to the back of the auditorium. Proscenium stages did not help, for the actors were up there in the picture-frame, divided from the front rows by an often wide and deep orchestra-pit. Directors, notably Robert Atkins at the Old Vic in the early twenties, tried to bring their players as far forward as possible, and to use as much direct address as they could,[18] whether by Lear, Iago, or Hamlet, Falstaff, or Launce, or Buckingham, or — as finely done in Peter Brook's production of *The Winter's Tale* (London, 1951) — by John Gielgud as Leontes. In spite of improvisations, everything was awkward while an orchestra

8*

pit remained. In the new theatre at Stratford-upon-Avon (opened 1932) there was a gulf between the stage and the front row of the stalls, and side walls were empty, without boxes. Indeed, the stage appeared sometimes to have only the barest communication with the audience. Baliol Holloway used to say that it was like acting to Boulogne from Folkestone. Robert Atkins in 1944–45, did his best to improve things; W. A. Darlington, astonished by the improvement in audibility at a revival of *The Merchant of Venice*, asked what had happened. 'Did you notice where I had hung my backcloth?' replied Atkins. 'Just two feet behind the proscenium arch. The whole play was set right out on the forestage.'[19] Yet problems have always remained, in spite of a strong improvement during a reconstruction in 1951 when the ends of the circle were taken round towards the stage, more as in the first Stratford theatre, though that was a horseshoe. Peter Hall, in 1963, was still grumbling about 'an obstinate proscenium stage with pieces stuck on the front'.

An orchestra pit was inevitable in any old British provincial theatre; the substantial brass rail went with the mirror-and-plush décor and seemed to be as permanent as the gilded plaster trophy above the proscenium arch. Today, in Britain, the Shakespeare songs are sung very rarely indeed to the accompaniment of a visible orchestra, as they were, for example, in Donald Wolfit's *As You Like It* at the Century Theatre, New York, as recently as the spring of 1947. Some directors, when they could, made a virtue of the orchestra pit. Harcourt Williams, in his Sadler's Wells *Julius Caesar* (1932) had 'two staircases from the pit (I used it as part of the Forum) which made the handling of the crowds much easier. Those staircases are no more but they have their counterparts in stone at the Wells. My memorial!'[20] Guthrie, in the Stratford-upon-Avon *Henry VIII* of 1949, let the Porter and his man on stage (V. iv) address the crowd in the pit which pelted them away. Something very like a custard pie was used and found its mark. David Buxton, in the Birmingham Repertory's jubilee revival (1963), had the crowd out of sight attempting to tug open one of the proscenium doors with which the theatre is equipped (there is no orchestra pit here). Elsewhere, Tyrrel — acted notably by Nehemiah Persoff — emerged from the pit to describe the murder of the Princes in a production of *Richard III* at Booth's Theatre, New York (1949); and this was done also, with uncanny effect, in the Budapest Madách Theatre's excitingly ingenious revival during 1969. Both Peter Brook (1950) and Anthony Quayle (1956) employed the pit as a lower level of the prison in *Measure For Measure* at Stratford. It was somewhere down there that Barnardine lay upon his rustling straw.

Probably no director of our period secured more intimacy with the simplest means than Robert Atkins did when in 1936–37 he made three productions, *Henry V, Much Ado About Nothing*, and *The Merry Wives of Windsor*, at a boxing stadium, the Ring, in Blackfriars. Here the audience sat round three-quarters of the building. The platform — in the ring itself — was backed by an imitation of the Elizabethan tiring-stage, with inner stage and balcony, and white light blazed upon the actors. Irene Vanbrugh, the Mistress Page of *The Merry Wives* — her sister, Violet, was Mistress Ford — had already played the part in unexpected surroundings. During 1934, Stanley Bell directed *The Merry Wives* at a variety theatre, the Manchester Hippodrome. According to Irene Vanbrugh:

> The centre of the auditorium which had served as a water tank in many of the variety bills, had the floor drawn over it and on top of this was spread a green carpet of artificial grass. Apart from one or two flats suggesting the entrance to the Pages' [Fords'] house, and on the other side the gallery of the Garter Inn, there was no scenery, and the play was staged on the village green. The audience sat all round and seemed to come right into the play with us . . .[21]

It was fun for the players but not for the box-office, and a week later the Hippodrome was re-opened as a music-hall, 'the green was removed, the sea-lions plunged into the tank, and the house was packed from floor to ceiling'.

Another resolute, popular, and lasting search for intimacy was in the procession down the aisle. True, Max Beerbohm, who could be tetchy, once complained, when the Chorus in Poel's production of *Samson Agonistes* came through the audience to reach the stage, that such a plan was ridiculous: 'Aesthetically, of course, there could be no reason for it since it must obviously destroy all aesthetic illusion and send us into paroxysms of internal laughter.'[22] Illusion was not noticeably destroyed when Russell Thorndike, as Touchstone, and his barefooted Audrey scampered up and down the aisles of Harvard University's staid Sanders Theatre (January 1931) during a Ben Greet production of *As You Like It*, decidedly in the Poel manner. There were impressive passages in the Federal Theatre's production of *Coriolanus* (Maxine Elliott, New York, 1938) when the mourning ladies of Rome approached the Volscian camp; and in the Princeton University Players' production (1950) when the tribunes, one on each side of the stage, addressed a mob in the two aisles, urging its vociferous members not to vote for Coriolanus.

Processions have been familiar at Stratford, Ontario, and during Edinburgh Festival Shakespeare. Occasionally, at the Edinburgh Assembly Hall, actors have seemed to be behind every door. Spectators in certain side seats have had to be careful with their feet. The late Eric Keown of *Punch*, a particularly tall man who needed leg-room, said once that he almost overturned Ophelia's funeral procession: 'Never put an unwary foot in the sceptred aisle.' Those having to leave early to catch a train during the *King John* of 1961 were embroiled with mourning monks. 'Masking' has often been a difficulty at Edinburgh after the processions have reached the stage: 'Very likely a Baron, or a Cardinal, or a man-at-arms, will be standing on, or by, the rim of the platform and obstructing our view. It is, on the whole, as awkward to see through a Cardinal as through Sam Weller's pair of stairs and a deal door.'[23]

Audiences at the Festival Theatre, Stratford, Ontario, have seen much, and often brilliant, processional and aisle work. A happy example occurred during *The Merry Wives of Windsor* in 1967, when Falstaff, as the old woman of Brentford, after dodging with surprising ability, was pursued from the stage, only to reappear and escape at last up the aisle of the theatre. Similar devices in other plays have been common at the Festival Theatre, Chichester, where directors seem able to find a use for every crevice of the building.

After the Second World War, an inevitable time-marker, there developed a steady preference for scenic suggestion against representation, for the hint rather than the hopeful illusion. Thus a single property, or group of properties, would say all that the designer and director wished to express: the dovecote and bit of wattle fence that announced Shallow's Cotswold manor in Stratford-upon-Avon's *2 Henry IV* (1951); Glen Byam Shaw's use of a hay-wain in the 1959 *King Lear* (IV. vi); the cart that seemed to be everlastingly with us during the 1964 historical cycle that Stratford called *The Wars of the Roses*; and the toy crusaders arrayed before the King in *2 Henry IV* during the same sequence.[24] From time to time there have been such symbols as the throne that dominated Stratford's 1951 tetralogy; the single star ('For I am constant as the Northern Star') that remained, from the Forum scene onwards, in Glen Byam Shaw's *Julius Caesar* (Stratford, 1957); and the remarkably telling Tarot card devices (Death, the wheel of Fortune, and so on), painted upon a screen, with two thrones to left and right, that formed the background of a *King John* at Goodhart Hall, Bryn Mawr College, Pennsylvania, in 1958 (director, Robert Butman). Indeed, symbols nowadays are expected: such things as the great cannon, far downstage, in Peter Hall's production of *Hamlet* (Stratford, 1965);[25] a whole sheaf in Stratford's 1969 season, notably the strained use, in various plays, of the Leonardo drawing of Renaissance Man; and, in the Prospect Players' *Richard II* (London, 1969–70), the stylized sun behind the throne and the crown above the stage.[26]

Numerous conventions are established. One is the scenic value of banners,[27] such as those in red, blue, and silver that formed the décor of Tyrone Guthrie's Coronation year production of *Henry V* (it holds the memory more than Olivier's later film); and the 'unfurling banners against spacious skies'[28] in Glen Byam Shaw's *Henry V* (Old Vic, 1951). Then, too, the direction of contests, or battles, in a stylized, almost hypnotic, slow motion. One thinks of the display before Simonides in *Pericles*, II. ii (Stratford, 1969) which rises simply from the direction, 'Great shouts within, and all cry "The mean knight!"'; the ballet-like fight at Bosworth, with its slow-waving banners, petrified archers, and soundless swordsmen, in *Richard III* (staged by Richard Barr, Booth's Theatre, New York, 1949); and the Roman-British battle in *Cymbeline*, V. ii (Peter Hall's production at Stratford-upon-Avon, 1957). This had a special visual quality, with its suggestion of a Roman phalanx — a wall of blazing copper shields — cutting through the British. Today the slow-motion battles must remind one inevitably of television's slow playback of a football goal or try. They are probably a reaction against the chaotic hurly-burly of film realism.

Lighting is now a complex part of most productions, natural at a time when the expert gets his special programme acknowledgement: it is long since those old touring company effects: morning, noon, and night switched on with an audible click. Now, with everything at their command, a few directors choose to ignore the switchboard and to keep to the unchanged light of the Elizabethan stage, though one may hazard that they are thinking in terms of Brecht rather than Shakespeare.

William Gaskill, in his Royal Court *Macbeth* (1966), with Alec Guinness and Simone Signoret, kept the light unvaried upon the bleak, brownish-papered box of his set. It is clear that Shakespeare himself strives to do all that we need ('There's husbandry in heaven, their candles are all out'; 'By the clock 'tis day, And yet dark night strangles the travelling lamp'; 'Light thickens, and the crow Makes wing to the rooky wood'; 'The west yet glimmers with some streaks of day'). Even so, the Royal Court stage looked curiously eccentric. One would have preferred the Benson way as reported by one of his last actors, R. Meadows White:[29] 'We always finished with two pans of red fire, one each side, out of sight, in front of the backcloth, so that the new Earls of Scotland hailed King Malcolm in billowing smoke and a ruby glare.'

Often a revival of *Romeo and Juliet* has been under-lighted: Karolos Koun's, for example, at Stratford in 1967. Nobody could accuse the young Peter Brook of this; though his 1947 *Romeo* was so much abused, it was always a Southern production. Bridges-Adams and Glen Byam Shaw would light their Stratford stages with a minimum of fuss. As with the permanent set, one should never be conscious of a manipulated switchboard; the changing atmospheric 'mood' lighting in the first part of *The Winter's Tale* (Stratford, 1969) jarred from the first: Leontes does not need this anxious emphasis. What one does want, and looks for — though hope is not invariably fulfilled — is for the lights to be kept down during the first moments of *Antony and Cleopatra* and then brought up in blaze on the great entry of the lovers, the world forgot: 'If it be love indeed, tell me how much' — 'There's beggary in the love that can be reckon'd.' It was among the final instructions Sir Barry Jackson gave to his Birmingham Repertory director, Bernard Hepton, and the revival of *Antony and Cleopatra* (February, 1961) was the last play Jackson saw in his own theatre.

Audiences at the Royal Shakespeare have come to expect

what is known now as 'Stratford smoke', usually swirling across a battlefield and cloaking the fighters, as in both recent productions of *Troilus and Cressida*: the Hall-Barton 'cockpit' revival of 1960 (Edinburgh, 1962) and the lesser, though much-bruited, Barton production of 1968. The effect can be exaggerated. It can, though, be used with creative imagination: one remembers the opening of the second scene of the Stratford-upon-Avon *Twelfth Night* (1969; director, John Barton). Here the stage, in a happy variation of the season's permanent set, dwindled away between painted walls, slatted and candle-lit, through a long perspective. Doors at the far end were thrown open, and Viola (Judi Dench), ushered in by a curl of white smoke like the foam-break of a wave, came slowly downstage, a figure entering a world of fantasy and uttering suddenly the romantic line, 'What country, friends, is this?'

It is increasingly obvious, however directors try to clear their stages, that audiences do want to see something. Even at Regent's Park in London, where the stage of the Open Air Theatre used to be left empty against its screen of poplar and sycamore and hazel, there has developed a fashion for architectural settings. True, Robert Atkins would occasionally use such an essential as the *Romeo and Juliet* balcony, or add a pavilion for *Pericles*; but we are now prepared to discover Portia's house at Belmont or Leonato's mansion agreeably designed but a benevolent superfluity in this particular setting. For Richard Digby Day's excellent productions of *The Merry Wives of Windsor* and *The Merchant of Venice* (1968) there was something like a tiring-house, with stairs to left and right.

We seldom get now the pure Poel austerity even in such a theatre as the Maddermarket at Norwich. There, under Poel's disciple, Nugent Monck, one noticed in *Pericles* (1951) the use of painted cloths: for some passages a stormy sea was shown at the back of the inner stage, and for others the deck of a ship was indicated above. As a complicated example of 'something to look at' one might choose the Stratford *Cymbeline* of 1962, a production — William Gaskill's — over which the shadow of Brecht hovered. The stage was framed in an off-white fish-net mesh that resembled rough and rucked knitting. Against it the designer, René Allio, either assembled bits and pieces of scenery or swung down a symbolic device from the flies. The battle was stylized. Posthumus was caged in a kind of chicken-coop. Among the artifices there were such streaks of naturalism as the carrying on of Cloten's severed head and Imogen's later mourning over a headless body grimly ensanguined. Having been asked to accept so much, one could have credited Cloten's fate without this splash of what Pooh-Bah, in quite another context, would call artistic verisimilitude.

We are still in an age of experiment, when anything can happen. So much depends on the individual director that the prophet stands aside.[30] One can merely go to any production with hope, though the bounty of a Brook *Titus Andronicus*, an Olivier performance of Othello, or Scofield's of Timon, must be rare indeed. It would be happier if directors refrained from discovering new significances that Shakespeare never dreamed about, struggling to make their productions unlike any other, and playing over and over the game of 'relevance to modern life' which can be both irrelevant and tedious.[31] Audiences are grateful for 'something to look at'. Most of all they appreciate the speaking of the text, 'the high unclouded summer of the word'. They do want the sound as well as the sense, and they respond instinctively to a performance of range and size. One observes a curious reluctance to 'give'; the Shakespeare stage needs more of the glory of fulfilment as well as the tremors of expectancy.[32] The best director must always be the man who abjures the programme note, keeps to the text, watches its orchestration — the 'march of music' said Shaw — and sees that his invention never minimizes the master in whose service he works.

Introduction

1. Henry Caine (1888–1962) to J. C. T. at St Ives, Cornwall, in August 1959.

2. Rupert Croft-Cooke, *The Drums of Morning*, London (1961), pp. 98–99: 'Henry Baynton . . . would take the centre of the stage, throw back his head, and recite "To be or not to be" as an opera singer lets fly an aria. But he had a splendid profile, a melodious voice, a presence, and a system of histrionics learnt in Frank Benson's company . . .' [In *As You Like It*] 'I can hear his words, spoken with that exaggerated hiss on the *s* which was a trick of elocution among Shakespearian actors of the time, like the pronunciation of "my" as very short "me" which I believe was supposed to sound like Elizabethan English.'

3. One remembers William Archer, *The Theatrical 'World' of 1897*, London (1898), p. 152, on Ben Greet's production at the Olympic in the summer of 1897: 'A roughly effective but topographically absurd representation of the Piazzetta and a corner of the Riva, with the Doge's Palace in the background . . . It finally appears that Shylock is the Doge's next-door neighbour.

4. Theatre Royal, Plymouth, 25 May 1922.

5. Donald Wolfit, *First Interval*, London (1954), p. 78.

6. I have seen the *Romeo and Juliet* double twice, in 1930 and 1956. On the former occasion it was performed at the Hollis Street Theatre, Boston, by Kenneth Wicksteed, with the company from Stratford. The comic Apothecary used sometimes to add to his exit:

> I will go a butcher's shop,
> And there I'll buy a mutton chop

(*Theatrical Inquisitor*, VIII, 1976 [20 April 1824]. Peter has always,

I believe, been the unnamed servant who cannot read, in Act I, scene ii.

7. King John, after the report that Arthur is still alive, will have 'the angry lords' meet in his closet (IV. ii. 266), and this is as unlikely to be a bedroom as the closet in which Dr Caius keeps his green box, and Simple hides, in *The Merry Wives of Windsor*, I. iv.

8. Gielgud's introduction to Rosamond Gilder, *John Gielgud's Hamlet*, New York and Toronto (1937), p. 64.

9. *He That Plays the King*, London, New York and Toronto (1950), p. 133.

10. Tyrone Guthrie, *A Life in the Theatre*, London (1959), p. 189.

11. Harley Granville-Barker, 'The Casting of Hamlet' in *The London Mercury*, November 1936.

12. Peter Dews in the Birmingham Repertory Theatre programme of *Hamlet*, March 1969: 'I have always responded more to a version of a Shakespeare play which didn't look like the last one.'

Chapter One: Stage Business

1. Acting edition (*c.* 1830) in Cumberland's *British Theatre*. In the same play Romeo's asking 'O me! What fray was here?' (I. i. 171) needs explanation. His catching sight of weapons left behind after the fighting does well enough and this has been the usual business from at least the 1880s.

2. See also Richard Sterne, *John Gielgud Directs Richard Burton in Hamlet*, London [1968], pp. 36, 71, 73.

3. Ben Greet in his acting edition of *The Merchant of Venice* mentions the number of ways in which Shylock's exit from the court can be made. He had seen 'a modern actor take about five minutes to get off' (Garden City, New York [1912], p. 166). Robert Helpmann's exit at the Old Vic in December 1956 was the most elaborate I can recall.

4. Sprague, *Shakespeare and the Actors* (1944), New York (Russell and Russell), 1963, pp. 197–200.

5. *Shakespeare and the Actors*, pp. 166–169, 197–200; and Sprague, *The Stage Business of Shakespeare's Plays: A Postscript*, London (Society for Theatre Research), 1954, pp. 19, 20, 28.

6. *The Manchester Stage, 1880–1900*, Westminster [1900], p. 66 (cf. *Shakespearian Stage Business*, p. 16).

7. Cf. A. Williamson, *Old Vic Drama 2*, London [1959], pp. 45, 46; and James Agate, *A Shorter Ego*, III, 196.

8. II. ii. 100. In 'transparent' he plays on the meaning 'brilliant', 'gloriously bright', as a tribute to her blonde beauty (Shakespeare, *Sixteen Plays*, ed. Kittredge, p. 187).

9. Press Cutting, 21 December 1960, in the Enthoven Collection (Old Vic folder).

10. No mention has been made of the business introduced at two points in *Hamlet*: in the Nunnery Scene when the Prince detects the presence of eavesdroppers; and during the narration of Ophelia's death, when her body is brought in (*Shakespeare and the Actors*, 152–154; 173). Practice at both points has varied greatly, even to there being no business at all.

Chapter Two: Cutting the Text

1. Basil Langton, at the Birmingham Repertory in 1942, used the same division. His *Hamlet* occupied two nights. On the first he would end after the Play; on the second he would repeat the Play scene and then continue to the end of the tragedy.

2. Clement Scott, *Some Notable Hamlets*, London (1900), p. 145.

3. Harcourt Williams, *Four Years at the Old Vic*, London (1935), p. 70.

4. Maurice Evans, in his so-called 'G.I.' *Hamlet* (1945), incredibly omitted both Gravediggers. The Second was omitted in a semi-professional production by the South Carolina Theatre at Fort Jackson, 21 November 1968 — A. C. S.

5. Arthur Colby Sprague, *The Doubling of Parts in Shakespeare's Plays*, London (1966), p. 25.

6. *Ibid.*, pp. 19–20, quoting the Boston *Sun*.

7. Programme of the Charles Doran provincial tours, 1922, in J. C. T.'s collection.

8. *The Times*, 15 January 1929.

9. James Agate, *Brief Chronicles*, London (1943), p. 216.

10. Hubert Griffith, *Iconoclastes: The Future of Shakespeare*, London (1928), p. 42.

11. G. K. Hunter, *Macbeth*, Penguin edition, London (1967), p. 39. Hunter says (p. 24), 'The court of Edward the Confessor, in contrast to the Witches' hovel, is a place of holy arts.'

12. Arthur Colby Sprague, in 'Shakespeare's Unnecessary Characters' (*Shakespeare Survey 20*: Cambridge, 1967) says that 'in modern productions when the Parthian episode is kept, it is with some risk of unintelligibility.'

13. Herbert Beerbohm Tree's note in the programme of his *Richard II*, His Majesty's Theatre, London 1903.

14. James Agate, *More First Nights*, London (1937), p. 70.

15. The *Birmingham Post*, 22 June, 1955.

16. Harley Granville-Barker, *Prefaces to Shakespeare*, London (1963 edition), Vol. III, p. 219.

17. *Ibid.*, Vol. II, p. 107.

18. Robert Speaight, *William Poel and the Elizabethan Revival*, London, (1954), p. 197.

19. The *Birmingham Post*, 13 March 1963.

20. H. Granville-Barker, *Prefaces to Shakespeare* (1963 edition), p. 90. These lines, he says, 'about touch bottom. Sheridan's burlesquing in *The Critic* has more life in it'.

Chapter Three: Additions to the Text

1. Henry Austin Clapp in The *Boston Advertiser*, 4 May 1897 (Blinn Scrapbooks in the Harvard Theatre Collection).

2. It may be significant that neither the added scene nor the new business was being employed in a production at Stratford in the spring of 1934 (cf. *The Shakespeare Pictorial* for May), but either or both may, of course, have been used earlier elsewhere.

3. Beerbohm Tree had included the 'Halt, halt,' in his production of the tragedy at His Majesty's Theatre in September 1911 (Dennis Bartholomeusz, *Macbeth and the Players*, Cambridge, 1969, p. 216).

4. *From 'The Bells' to 'King Arthur'*, London (1896), p. 234. Rosaline is mentioned in the cast and in Irving's acting edition.

5. Odell, '*A Midsummer Night's Dream* on the New York Stage', *Shakespearean Studies*, New York (1916).

6. J. B. Wright's Broadway Theatre Promptbook, 1854, in the Becks Collection.

7. Lady Benson, *Mainly Players*, London (1936), p. 80.

8. Harold Hobson, *Theatre*, London (1948), p. 140. There is a temptation to exploit the Indian, once he has been allowed to appear as a character. Robert Atkins is commended by *Punch* for the exuberance of his direction. 'We even see Puck (Mr Leslie French) kidnap the little changeling boy whose custody caused so much trouble' (21 August 1935).

Chapter Four: Speaking the Lines

1. James Agate, *More First Nights*, London (1937), p. 344.

2. J. C. Trewin, *A Play Tonight*, London (1952), pp. 154–155; and *Shakespeare on the English Stage: 1900–1964*, London (1964), p. 223

3. This is indicated as far back as Ben Greet's acting edition in 1912.

4. Arthur Colby Sprague, *Shakespeare's Histories: Plays for the Stage*, London (1964), p. 40.

5. George Skillan, *King Lear* edition, London (1967), p. 182; note 179.

6. Hugh Hunt, *Old Vic Prefaces*, London (1954), pp. 98–99.

7. Baliol Holloway wrote in a letter to James Agate (1936): 'I think that I can trace why Armado was regarded as a good part. Phelps elected to play it in his own production at Sadler's Wells —

and he was too much of a gentleman to swop it for Costard on the second performance.'

8. Granville-Barker, *Prefaces to Shakespeare*, London (1963 edition), Vol. II, p. 160.

9. Arthur Colby Sprague, *Shakespeare's Histories: Plays for the Stage*, London (1964), p. 63.

10. Michael Redgrave (New, 1950) preferred 'Woo't drink up Nilus? eat a crocodile?' to the more familiar 'eisel' at *Hamlet*, V. i. 70.

11. See the text as printed in Richard L. Sterne's book, *John Gielgud Directs Richard Burton in Hamlet: A Journal of Rehearsals*, New York (1967).

12. The *Sketch*, 29 March 1950.

13. Arthur Colby Sprague, *Shakespeare and the Actors: The Stage Business in His Plays (1660–1905)*, Harvard (1945), p. 16.

14. Laurence Irving, *Henry Irving: The Actor and His World*, London (1951), p. 403.

Chapter Five: Sights and Sounds

1. *The Shakespearean Scene*, London, etc. (1949), pp. 20, 21. See also *Oscar Asche: His Life*, London (1929), p. 136; *The Athenaeum*, 4 March 1911; and Charles Shattuck (ed.), *The Merry Wives of Windsor*, 'Laurel Shakespeare', New York (1966), pp. 35–38.

2. Lawrence Thompson, *Behind the Curtain: An Introduction to the Theatre*, London and Melbourne (1951), p. 70.

3. The distinction is one which Mr Shaw stresses in a recent letter, appealing to his own experience at Stratford in 1952, 'when there was heavy snow on the ground as the company were beginning rehearsals and a most beautiful spring day when the play opened'.

4. *The Times*, 17 June 1924. Why is it that Helena in *All's Well That Ends Well* who, in her pilgrim dress, should be barefooted (III. iv. 6) never is?

5. See, e.g., the Rowe 1714 plate of Falstaff at Gadshill; and the curious engraving of Falstaff at Shrewsbury, discussed by Christian P. Gruber in *Theatre Notebook* XXI (1967), 120, 121.

6. 'How Fat Was Falstaff?' *Punch*, 27 February 1946.

7. *Westminster Gazette*, 21 September 1921 (Carroll Press Cuttings Book in the Enthoven Collection, Victoria and Albert Museum).

8. Cf. G. B. Harrison's stage direction in his 'New Reader's Shakespeare' and J. L. Styan, *Shakespeare's Stagecraft*, Cambridge (1967), p. 35.

9. Promptbook, dated 1864, marked by George Becks. For the identification, see Charles Shattuck, *The Shakespeare Promptbooks*, Urbana, Illinois (1965), p. 473. See Max Beerbohm on Tree's nightcap (His Majesty's, 1901) in *More Theatres: 1898–1903*, London (1969), p. 349.

10. Raymond Mander and Joe Mitchenson, *Hamlet through the Ages*, Melbourne, London and Toronto (1955), pp. 111, 112. See also the *Evening Standard* and the *Daily Telegraph*, 26 April 1928, on Jean Forbes-Robertson at the Old Vic (Carroll Press Cuttings Book).

11. For the stage Paris, cf. Hugh Hunt, *Old Vic Prefaces*, London (1954), p. 127.

12. The first is in the Mander and Mitchenson Collection; the other two in the Shakespeare Memorial Library, Birmingham.

13. *Shakespeare's Use of Off-Stage Sounds*, Lincoln, Nebraska (1963).

14. *Ibid.*, 116 note. Miss Jeanne Newlin calls my attention to a terrifying picture in the *Illustrated Sporting and Dramatic News*, 23 September 1876, of the lightning flash as it was simulated in a contemporary production at Liverpool.

15. This effect of Calvert's 'which brought the audience to their feet', is lauded by Alfred Darbyshire: 'That peal of thunder cost weeks of thought and mechanical labour; it was no mere stage thunder'. (*An Architect's Experience*, Manchester, 1897, p. 315).

Chapter Six: The People of the Plays

1. In 'The Social Background,' included in *A Companion to Studies*, edited by Harley Granville-Barker and G. B. Harrison, Cambridge (1934), p. 210.

2. The *Birmingham Post*, 2 April 1958.

3. *Ibid.*, 23 April 1958.

4. Promptbook of *Twelfth Night*, John Harrison's production, Birmingham Repertory Theatre, March 1966.

5. Preface to *Twelfth Night*, Savoy Theatre acting edition (London, 1912), p. ix.

6. Hugh Hunt, *Old Vic Prefaces*, London (1954), p. 77.

7. London (1954), p. 23.

8. Promptbook of *Twelfth Night*, Birmingham Repertory, March 1966.

9. 'When anybody spoke to him it seemed minutes before a faint glimmering appeared in the eye like the promise of daybreak.' — *International Theatre Annual No. 3*, London (1958), p. 198.

10. *Punch*, 19 July 1944.

11. The *Illustrated London News*, 23 April 1955.

12. Hugh Hunt, *Old Vic Prefaces*, London (1954), p. 74.

13. James Agate, *Brief Chronicles*, London (1943), p. 26.

14. The *Birmingham Post*, 25 April 1958.

15. T. C. Kemp, *The Stratford Festival*, Birmingham (1953), p. 190.

16. J. Agate, *The Contemporary Theatre, 1923*, London (1924) p. 99.

17. *The Observer*, 19 September 1948.

18. The *Birmingham Post*, 18 May 1960. Jonathan Miller has been unkinder to Feste than any other director in memory. When he staged the play (1969) for the Oxford and Cambridge Shakespeare Company, he decided that the jester was a vinegary and unmusical hack.

19. Preface to *A Midsummer Night's Dream*, Savoy Theatre acting edition (London), 1914, pp. vii–viii.

20. *International Theatre Annual No. 3*, London (1958), p. 202.

21. *The Spectator*, 18 December 1920.

22. J. Agate, *The Contemporary Theatre, 1923*, London (1924), pp. 202–203.

23. J. Agate, *The Contemporary Theatre*, 1924, London (1925), p. 63.

24. Herbert Farjeon, *The Shakespearean Scene*, London (1949), p. 47.

25. Harcourt Williams, *Four Years at the Old Vic*, London (1935), p. 54.

26. J. C. Trewin, *A Play Tonight*, London (1952), p. 156.

27. Harcourt Williams, *Four Years at the Old Vic*, London (1935), p. 123. Arthur Colby Sprague points out in *Shakespeare's Histories:*

Plays for the Stage, London (1964), p. 109, that 'in Holinshed Shakespeare would have found references to the French monarch's "old disease of frenzie" and to " his old frantike disease", but there is no trace of his having put this idea to use.'

28. Arthur Colby Sprague, *Shakespeare's Histories: Plays for the Stage*, London (1964), p. 105.

29. Herbert Farjeon, *The Shakespearean Scene*, London (1949), p. 88.

30. John Gielgud, *Stage Directions*, London (1963), p. 33.

31. Quoted in *Granville Barker* by C. B. Purdom, London (1955), p. 253. Perhaps the best York of our time — and never for a moment a near–Polonius — has been Robert Eddison in the Cottrell production for Prospect Players (1969–70).

32. Gordon Crosse, *Shakespearean Playgoing: 1890–1952*, London (1955), p. 130. At Stratford in 1964 Roy Dotrice was red-haired, kilted, and Border-accented.

33. Arthur Colby Sprague, *Shakespeare's Histories: Plays for the Stage*, London (1964), p. 57. J. C. Trewin, *We'll Hear a Play*, London (1949), pp. 24–25.

34. The *Illustrated London News*, 14 May 1955.

35. The *Birmingham Post*, 23 February 1960.

36. *Hamlet*, New Cambridge edition, edited by J. Dover Wilson, Cambridge (1934), p. 253.

37. Norman Marshall, *The Producer and the Play*, London (1962 edition), p. 193.

38. Hugh Hunt, *Old Vic Prefaces*, London (1954), p. 48.

39. Clement Scott, *Some Notable Hamlets*, London (1900), p. 172.

40. *Ibid.*, p. 193.

41. Herbert Farjeon, *The Shakespearean Scene*, London (1949), p. 150.

42. James Agate, *Brief Chronicles*, London (1943), p. 58. In his *Sunday Times* notice (13 April 1924), he wrote: 'What, by the way, was the Shakespearian meaning of the word "convenient"? Balthazar said, "Madam, I go with all convenient speed," and dawdled off like a snail. But shouldn't he have gone with "appropriate" speed — that is, quickly — as he was commanded?' Allan Wilkie did not make Balthazar comic.

43. Hugh Hunt, *Old Vic Prefaces*, London (1954), p. 161.

Chapter Seven: Stages and Staging

1. W. Bridges-Adams, *The British Theatre*, London (1944), p. 46.

2. See Arthur Colby Sprague, *Shakespearian Players and Performances*, London (1954), p. 151.

3. In *Julius Caesar* (Old Vic, 1962), the designer, Nicholas Georgiadis, 'objecting to a gleaming marmoreal Rome of bath-towel togas, saw the city as a place of rough and rusty scaffolding with its citizens most shabbily arrayed. One kept on thinking of rust, an illusion helped by the colour of the sky. . . . The set called up other things as well: skeletons imperfectly articulated, and a housing project in the rain'. — *Shakespeare Quarterly* (Autumn, 1962), p. 509.

4. 11 January 1900.

5. W. Bridges-Adams, *The British Theatre*, London (1944), p. 46: 'More . . . a suggestive influence than a creative force.'

6. The *Birmingham Post*, 11 April 1956.

7. J. C. Trewin, *Shakespeare on the English Stage 1900–1964*, London (1964), p. 244.

8. W. Bridges-Adams, *The British Theatre*, London (1944), p. 34.

9. 'The wit is ironical and the melodrama is perfectly serious. To smother them both with slapstick is not only to destroy the substance of your play but to invite your play to answer back. . . . It did so pretty sharply, and the result was the most spectacular suicide I have ever seen in the theatre.' — Robert Speaight in *Shakespeare Quarterly* (Autumn, 1965), p. 313.

10. Archibald Haddon, *Green Room Gossip*, London (1922), p. 63.

11. Old ways can linger. Annibale Ninchi's Italian company had five intervals in its *Hamlet* at the Orpheum Theatre, Gzira, Malta, in January 1952. They were long intervals, too. — A. C. S.

12. Recalled by Sprague in *Shakespearian Players and Performances*, p. 168.

13. Prologue for the Shakespeare performances at the British Theatre Exhibition, Birmingham, 1949.

14. 'Unaltered except for a number of imperceptible light cues that varied in emphasis.' — M. St Clare Byrne in Vol. 2 of her edition of Granville-Barker's *Prefaces to Shakespeare*, London (1963).

9

From this production one thinks of the appearance of the characters in the opening scene (Norfolk, Buckingham, Abergavenny) while Prologue was still speaking.

15. Speaking of this set in *Shakespearian Players and Performances*, p. 213, Sprague says: 'The more formal the setting, the more readily it can be shaped to the imagination'. Scott's design served equally well for Verona and Milan, but there was a certain difficulty at the end of the play when, in the same setting, Valentine had to speak of 'this shadowy desert, unfrequented woods'.

16. The *Illustrated London News*, 5 September 1964.

17. Sir Tyrone Guthrie, *A Life in the Theatre*, London (1960), p. 109.

18. The Herald in *Othello*, II. i, 'It is Othello's pleasure; our noble and valiant general . . .,' should certainly address us (there is no 'crowd following' in early stage directions) and in many productions this has worked well. — A. C. S.

19. W. A. Darlington, *Six Thousand and One Nights*, London (1960), p. 197.

20. Harcourt Williams, *Old Vic Saga*, London (1949), p. 117.

21. Dame Irene Vanbrugh, *To Tell My Story*, London (1948), pp. 142–143.

22. Sir Max Beerbohm, *Around Theatres*, London (1953 edition), p. 531. Quoted in Sprague, *Shakespearian Players and Performances*, London (1954), p. 147. The performance of *Samson Agonistes* was in December 1908, at Burlington House, London.

23. *Shakespeare Quarterly* (Autumn, 1962), p. 505.

24. 'The voyage to the Holy Land — never to be realized — was brilliantly emphasized by the gaunt, overhanging Crucifix and the toy paladins on the floor.' — Robert Speaight in *Shakespeare Quarterly* (Autumn, 1964), p. 384.

25. See Martin Holmes, *The Guns of Elsinore*, London (1964), p. 181.

26. *Birmingham Post*, 27 August 1969: 'That tale of death within the hollow crown.'

27. See Sprague, *Shakespeare's Histories: Plays for the Stage*, London (1964), p. 97.

28. Trewin, *A Play Tonight*, London (1952), p. 77.

29. Quoted in *Benson and the Bensonians*, London (1960), p. 256.

30. Arthur Colby Sprague, in *Shakespearian Players and Performances*, pp. 147 and 211, quoses two phrases from a letter Bernard Shaw contributed to Joseph Harker's *Studio and Stage*, London (1924): 'The stage for which he [Shakespeare] wrote his plays is the only one to which they are adapted, and on which they make the effects he planned'; 'The principle must be applied with constant regard to common sense and knowledge of essential points.'

31. Cf. Gareth Llloyd Evans, in *Shakespeare Survey 22*, Cambridge (1969).

32. *Flourish* (London), Summer 1969, p. 7.

Index of Persons

Abbot, John, 94
Adrian, Max, 49, 97
Agate, James, 40, 81
    quoted, 42, 66, 95, 96, 98, 99,
        105, 133 note
Aherne, Brian, 31
Albertazzi, Giorgio, 24
Alexander, Sir George, 82
Allio, René, 123
Anderson, Mary, 90
Arundal, Dennis, 66
Arche, Oscar, 18
    produces *As You Like It*, 77,
        78
Ashcroft, Dame Peggy, 75, 79
    as Titania, 65
Atkins, Robert, 45, 86, 96, 122
    as a director, 16, 115, 116, 117
    directs *Midsummer Night's
        Dream*, 34, 99, 129 note
    quoted, 116
Atkinson, Brooks
    quoted, 79
Ayrton, Randle, 68, 87

Badel, Alan, 68
Bannen, Ian, 24, 58
Barbour, James
    as Shylock, 55, 56
Barr, Richard, 120

Barrault, Jean-Louis, 65
Barrymore, John, 19
    as Hamlet, 31, 104
Barton, John, 74
    directs *Twelfth Night*, 122
Bates, Michael,
    as Touchstone, 90
Baynton, Henry, 11, 12, 14, 16, 19,
        105
    acting described, 13, 16, 125
        note
Beerbohm, Max
    quoted, 118
Bell, Stanley, 105, 117
Benson, Sir Frank, 11, 14, 15, 20,
        36, 38, 41, 46, 47, 48, 64,
        100, 121
    as Malvolio, 84
    produces entirety *Hamlet*, 37, 38
Benson Company, 11, 72, and
        passim
Benthall, Michael
    directs *Antony and Cleopatra*, 41
    — *As You Like It*, 79
    — *Hamlet*, 32, 33
    — *Midsummer Night's Dream*, 33,
        34, 109
Betterton, Thomas, 25
Birch, Frank, 83
Booth, Edwin, 16, 30, 31

Brecht, B., 107, 120, 123
Bridges-Adams, W., 16, 36, 68, 75, 93, 99, 109, 121
  directs *I Henry IV*, 34, 73
  — *Henry V*, 111
  — *Richard II*, 42, 112
  — *The Tempest*, 109
  quoted, 134 note
Brook, Lesley, 96
Brook, Peter, 47, 74, 109, 114, 115, 117, 123
  directs *Romeo and Juliet*, 47, 121
Brown, Ivor, 81, 112
Brown, John Russell, 21
Brown, Pamela, 61
Browne, Coral, 98
Brydone, Alfred, 100
Burrell, John
  directs *Richard III*, 61
Burton, Richard, 32, 73
Butman, Robert
  directs *King John*, 119
Buxton, David, 116, 117
Byford, Roy, 54
Byrne, M. St Clare, 92, 134 note

Caine, Henry
  quoted, 12
Calvert, Charles
  produces *Henry V*, 51
  — *Winter's Tale*, 91, 131 note
Carey, Denis, 113
Carten, Audrey, 98
Casson, Sir Lewis, 40, 43
Churchyard, Thomas, 59
Cibber, Colley
  see *Richard III*
Clarke, Nigel, 100
Clinton-Baddeley, V. C.
  quoted on Myrmidons, 82, 83
Clunes, Alec, 53
Coates, Wells, 114, 115

Coghill, Nevill, 63
  quoted on Indian boy, 64, 65
Cooper, Frederick, 104
Cottrell, Richard, 43
Craig, Gordon, 108, 134 note
Crosse, Gordon
  quoted, 102

Dale, John, 84
Daly, Augustin, 51, 64, 79
  directs *Much Ado*, 52
Darbyshire, Alfred, 131 note
Darch, Frank, 13
Darlington, W. A., 116
Davenant, Sir William
  see *Macbeth*
Day, Richard Digby, 122
  directs *Merchant of Venice*, 47, 122
Dean, Basil, 98
Deeter, Jasper, 28
Dench, Judi, 122
Dent, Alan
  quoted, 58
Devine, George, 55
Dews, Peter
  quoted, 126 note
Dignam, Mark, 18
Dillon, Charles, 29
Dixon, Adéle, 39
Doran, Charles, 12, 13, 14, 15, 20, 39, 84
  as Malvolio, 84
  Company, 11, 15, 16, 105
Dotrice, Roy
  as Hotspur, 133 note
Duncan, Frank
  as Young Percy, 102
Dunlop, Frank, 111
Dunstan, Edward, 12

Eddison, Robert, 101
  as Feste, 96, 97
  — Polonius

Elliott, Michael, 19
Elton, Oliver, 31
Evans, Dame Edith,
  as Helena, 98, 99
Evans, Maurice, 127 note
  as Falstaff, 28, 80, 81
  — Richard II, 42, 66, 101
Eyre, Ronald, 47

Fagan, J. B., 98
Farjeon, Herbert, 78, 101
  quoted, 99
Forbes-Robertson, Jean, 131 note
Forbes-Robertson, Sir Johnston,
  104
  as Hamlet, 31, 37
  bowdlerizes Othello, 45
ffrangcon-Davies, Gwen, 100
French, Leslie, 16, 69, 96, 129
  note

Gaskill, William, 121
  directs Cymbeline, 123
Georgiadis, Nicholas
  setting for Julius Caesar, 134
  note
Gielgud, Sir John, 19, 32, 42, 69,
  73, 102, 115
  as Benedick, 75
  — Hamlet, 24, 32, 73
  quoted on Duke of York, 101
Glossop-Harris, Florence, 12
Granville-Barker, Harley, 16, 50,
  51, 71, 87, 108, 109, 111
  quoted 20, 43, 44, 93, 94, 96, 97,
  98, 102, 128 note
Goring, Marius, 97
Greet, Sir Philip Ben, 12, 13, 17,
  36, 71, 80, 96, 129 note
  produces As You Like It, 118
  — Merchant of Venice, 125 note
  quoted, 105, 126 note

Grey, Earle, 72
Griffith, Hubert, 40
Guinness, Sir Alec, 96, 121
  as Reynaldo, 38
  production of Hamlet, 90
Guthrie, Sir Tyrone, 38, 46, 63,
  68, 95, 99, 113, 120
  directs All's Well, 52
  — Henry VIII, 113, 115, 134
  note
  — Troilus and Cressida, 111
  quoted, 20, 21, 94, 114, 115
Gwynn, Michael
  as Duke of York, 102

Haddon, Archibald
  quoted, 111, 112
Hall, Peter, 40, 58, 95, 110, 120,
  122
  directs Cymbeline, 44, 114, 120
Hampden, Walter, 56
Hampton, Richard, 24
Hands, Terry, 70
Hardy, Robert, 18, 73, 102
Harris, Rosemary, 65
Harrison, John, 66, 67
  directs Twelfth Night, 49, 93, 94
Hauser, Frank
  directs Antony and Cleopatra, 112
Hayes, George, 69
Helpmann, Robert, 126 note
  directs Antony and Cleopatra, 41
Henderson, John, 72
Hepton, Bernard, 103, 121
Herbert, Henry, 14
Heywood, Thomas, 59
Holloway, Baliol, 102
  as Don Armado, 70, 129 note
  quoted, 116, 129 note
Howard, Alan, 75, 76
Howard, Leslie, 24
Howe, George, 101

Hudd, Walter, 58
Hunt, Hugh, 70
    directs *Twelfth Night*, 93, 94, 95, 96, 97
    quoted, 104, 105, 106
Hunt, Martita, 99
Hunter, G. K.
    quoted on *Macbeth*, 40, 128 note
Hurry, Leslie, 113, 114

Irving, H. B., 11, 12
    as Don John, 82
Irving, Sir Henry, 31, 75, 104
    addition to *The Merchant of Venice*, 55, 56
    production of *Romeo and Juliet*, 59
Isham, Gyles, 102

Jackson, Sir Barry, 43, 103, 115, 121
James, Finlay, 115
Jefford, Barbara
    as Isabel, 74
Jewett, Henry, 90

Kean, Charles, 42, 52, 100
    produces *Midsummer Night's Dream*, 64
    — *Richard II*, 51
Kean, Mrs Charles, 100
Kean, Edmund, 23
Kemble, John Philip, 23
    acting edition of *King John*, 27
    — of *Othello*, 30
Kemble, Stephen,
    as Falstaff, 28
Keown, Eric
    quoted, 118, 119
Kidd, John, 102
Kirkman, Francis,
    The Wits, 80
Kittredge, G. L., 127 note

Komisarjevsky, Theodore, 69, 71, 109
Koun, Karolos, 121

Lang, Matheson, 84, 102
    as Voltimand, 37
Langham, Michael, 52
    directs *Hamlet*, 109, 110
    — *Henry V*, 112
    — *Midsummer Night's Dream*, 34
Langton, Basil
    directs 'entirety' *Hamlet*, 127 note
Lauchlan, Agnes, 99
Leiber, Fritz, 56, 108
Leigh, Andrew, 39, 40, 45
Leighton, Margaret, 79
Littlewood, Joan, 113, 114
Livesey, Roger, 100

McCowen, Alec, 71
McEwan, Geraldine
    as Olivia, 95
McKern, Leo, 96
Macready, William Charles, 23, 100
    production of *As You Like It*, 90
Machen, Arthur,
    quoted, 41
Mantell, Robert, B., 12 note
    company, 16, 56
Marsh, Alexander, 12, 13
Martin-Harvey, Sir John, 38
    as Osric, 104
    directs *Taming of the Shrew*, 54
Miller, Jonathan, 132 note
Milton, Ernest, 13, 15, 70
Moisilwitsch, Tanya, 113, 115
Monck, Nugent
    directs *Pericles*, 44, 45, 122
    — *Taming of the Shrew*, 55
Morley, Christopher, 115

Muller, Robert, 34

Napier, Frank, 45, 101
Neilson, Harold V., 12, 15
Neilson, Julia, 82, 108
Neilson-Terry, Phyllis
   as Olivia, 95
Neville, John, 24, 103
   as Sir Andrew, 94, 132 note
Neville, Oliver, 40
Newcombe, Mary
   as Duchess of York in *Richard II*,
      42
Newlin, Jean, 131
Nicholson, H. O., 93
   as Starveling, 67
Ninchi, Annibale, 134 note
Nobili, Lila de, 114
Noguchi, Isamu, 111
Nunn, Trevor
   directs *Much Ado*, 75, 76

Olivier, Sir Lawrence, 32, 38, 41,
      43, 45, 56, 61, 66, 74, 120,
      123
   as Hamlet, 66, 113
   — Hotspur, 81, 102, 103
   — Malvolio, 94, 95
Otway, Thomas,
   Don Carlos, 26

Pasco, Richard, 24
Paul, Mrs Howard
   as Hecate and Lady Macbeth,
      39
Payne, B. Iden, 49, 54
   as director, 109
Persoff, Nehemiah, 117
Phelps, Samuel, 129 note
Poel, William, 16, 49, 51, 101, 109,
      118
   as director, 45, 108

Porter, Neill, 15, 66

Quayle, Anthony, 31, 42, 43, 102,
      117

Redgrave, Sir Michael, 100, 102,
      130 note
Redgrave, Vanessa, 80
Richardson, Sir Ralph, 15, 32
   as Falstaff, 81
Richardson, Tony, 30, 39
Richmond Shakespeare Society
   production of *I Henry IV*, 34
   — of *Richard III*, 61
Roberts, Oswald Dale, 9
Robeson, Paul, 89
Rodway, Norman, 49
Rogers, Paul, 68, 69
Rowe, Nicholas, 26
Rutherfurd, Tom, 32

St Barbe-West, Miss,
   as Audrey, 80
Salpeter, Max, 45
Scofield, Paul, 32, 40, 44, 123
Scott, Clement
   quoted, 37, 38, 59, 104
Scott, Harold, 87
Scott, Hutchinson
   setting for *Two Gentlemen of
      Verona*, 113, 135 note
Scott, Margaretta, 66
Seale, Douglas, 43, 78, 111
   directs *Henry V*, 53
   — *1–3 Henry VI*, 115
Seyler, Athene
   as Hermia, 98
Sharp, Anthony
   as Malvolio, 58
Sharpe, Edith, 15

Shaw, Glen Byam, 53, 119, 120, 121
  directs *As You Like It*, 78–80, 88
  quoted, 130 note
Shelley, Norman, 15
Shepherd, Elizabeth, 63
Sheppard, Harry, 28
Shridan, R. B.
  The Critic, 89, 108, 128 note
Shirley, Francis, 88
Shuttleworth, Bertram,
  as Peter Quince, 87
Signoret, Simone, 121
Skillan, George, 86
  acting edition of *1 Henry IV*, 34
  — of *King Lear*, 70
Slater, Daphne, 96
Sofaer, Abraham, 15
Speaight, Robert, 45
  quoted, 110, 134 note, 135 note
Spriggs, Elizabeth,
  as Mrs Quickly, 103
Stamm, Rudolf, 21
Stride, John, 100
Sullivan, Barry, 16, 66, 73
Sullivan, John, 105
Suzman, Janet, 75, 76
Swirley, Ian, 66

Tearle, Sir Godfrey, 31, 89, 108
Terry, Ellen, 75
Thesiger, Ernest, 94
Thomas, Gwevril, 39
Thompson, Lawrence
  quoted, 79
Thorndike, Dame Sybil, 43, 100
Thorndike, Russell, 118
Thorpe-Bates, Peggy, 43
Townsend, Genevieve, 14, 18

Tree, Sir Herbert Beerbohm, 14, 51, 80, 84, 102, 107, 108, 109, 110, 129, 131 note
  as *Hamlet*, 24, 37
  directs *King John*, 52
  — *Much Ado*, 46
  — *Richard II*, 42
Tree, Viola, 96
Trevor, Austin, 82
Tynan, Kenneth, 19

Valère, Simone, 65
Vanbrugh, Irene
  quoted, 117
Vanbrugh, Violet, 117
Vandenhoff, John, 100
Vaughan, Stuart, 61

Waller, David, 49
Walter, Wilfrid, 75
Warner, David, 24
Webster, Margaret, 42, 69, 89
  directs *1 Henry IV*, 28, 35
  — *Macbeth*, 57
Whitby, Arthur, 87
White, R. Meadows
  quoted, 121
Whitty, Dame May, 32
Wickham, Glynne, 63
Wicksteed, Kenneth, 13, 69, 125 note
  as Peter Quince, 86, 87
Wilkie, Allan, 57, 86, 133 note
  quoted on *As You Like It*, 18, 19
Williams, Clifford
  directs *Comedy of Errors*, 71, 72
Williams, Harcourt, 38, 39, 40, 42, 43, 45, 54, 69, 99
  as French King in *Henry V*, 106
  quoted, 116
Williamson, Nicol
  as Hamlet, 39

Wilson, J. D., 19, 73, 103, 104
  quoted, 28
Wolfit, Sir Donald, 11, 15, 18, 31, 116
  as Malvolio, 58, 84
Wood, Edward J., 13
Worth, Irene,
  as Helena, 99

Wrede, Gaspar, 44
Wreford, Edgar, 101
Wynyard, Diana, 75

Zefferelli, G. Franco, 110, 111
  directs *Romeo and Juliet*, 32, 58, 59, 110

Index of Plays

All's Well that Ends Well, 29
  added scene, 52
  Helena's costume, 130 note
Antony and Cleopatra, 12, 110, 112
  Act III, scene i, 41, 43, 49, 112,
    128 note
  Clown, 69
  minor characters combined, 41
  opening scene, 121
  Ventidius (*see* Act III, scene i)
As You Like It, 12, 13, 69, 116, 125
    note
  Audrey, 80, 83, 88, 90, 118
  costumes of actresses, 80, 118
  cuts, 46
  off-stage sounds, 90
  properties, 80, 88
  seasonal change, 14, 77, 78–80,
    130 note
  setting of scenes, 14, 18, 19, 113

Catherine and Petruchio, 88
Comedy of errors, 12, 71
  Baynton's version, 13
  treatment of lines, 71, 72
Coriolanus, 12
  cuts, 41, 43
  Spy Scene, 41, 43, 44
  staging of scenes, 118
  treatment of lines, 66

Cymbeline, 12, 123
  Apparitions, 41, 44
  Cloten, 71, 123 note
  cuts, 41, 44, 45, 50
  Gaoler Scene, 44
  setting, 114

Hamlet, 12, 13, 15, 18, 23, 109, 113,
    115, 118, 120, 125 note
  Act IV, scene iii, 51
  altered lines, 73, 130 note
  beginning, 89, 90
  business, 17, 21, 22, 23, 24, 26,
    27, 31, 32, 33, 127 note
  Closet Scene, 16, 19, 26, 27
  costumes, 15, 17, 84, 85, 111
  cuts, 13, 37–39, 49, 127 note
  doubling of parts, 17, 18
  'entirety' productions, 37, 127
    note
  first Quarto, 17
  Fortinbras ending, 13, 37, 38
  Gravediggers, 14, 17, 69, 127
    note
  Mad Scene, 84, 85
  off-stage sound, 89, 90
  Olivier film, 38
  Osric, 97, 103, 104
  pictures, 26, 27
  Polonius, 17, 18, 21, 22, 88

Hamlet,—contd.
  Prayer Scene, 32, 33
  properties, 19, 24, 88
  Reynaldo, 13, 38
  setting of scenes, 13, 14, 19
  treatment of lines, 22, 66, 67, 71,
    72, 73
1 Henry IV, 88, 113, 114, 115
  added words, 55
  Falstaff discovered in I, 2, 27, 28
  Falstaff's costume, 80, 81, 83,
    130 note
  Hotspur, 81, 102, 103, 133 note
  Play Scene, 72, 73
  Mrs Quickly, 35, 97, 103
  Second Tavern Scene, 34, 35
2 Henry IV, 113, 114, 119
  Falstaff's costume (see *1 Henry
    IV*)
  Mrs Quickly (see *1 Henry IV*)
  season, 77
  setting of scenes, 119, 135 note
Henry V, 12, 15, 111, 112, 117, 120
  added scenes, 51, 52, 53, 56,
    note
  Archbishop's exposition, 46
  business, 53, 56, 100, 128 note
  Chorus, 46, 100, 101, 111, 113
  cuts, 46
  French King, 97, 100, 133 note
  Henry's ruthlessness explained,
    53
  Pistol and Fluellen, 65, 101
  transposition of scenes, 49, 50,
    101
  treatment of lines, 70, 71, 72
1–3 Henry VI, 115
1 Henry VI
  cuts, 41
Henry VIII, 113, 115, 134 note
  setting of scenes, 113, 116

Julius Caesar, 12, 51
  Cinna the Poet, 13, 46
  cuts, 13, 46, 47
  intrusive poet, 47
  setting of scenes, 108, 116, 119,
    134 note
  treatment of lines, 71

King John, 118, 119, 126 note
  Austria's head, 27
  Magna Charta, 52
  re-arrangement by Kemble, 27
  treatment of lines, 70
King Lear, 12, 88, 109, 111, 115
  business, 17
  Edgar, 70
  Oswald and Kent, 17
  setting, 114, 119

Love's Labour's Lost, 12, 79, 109
  Don Armado, 70, 74
  ending, 73, 74
  treatment of lines, 73, 74

Macbeth, 12, 13, 109, 121
  added words, 57, 129 note
  business of dropping the cup, 25
  costumes, 15
  cuts, 13, 39, 40
  Davenant's version, 57
  doubling, 39
  English Doctor, 13, 40, 128 note
  Hecate, 39, 40
  off-stage sounds, 57, 88
  setting of scenes, 14, 15
  treatment of lines, 66, 67, 71
Measure for Measure, 12, 62
  Kate Keepdown, 61–63
  Lucio, 62, 63
  Pompey, 63
  setting of scenes, 117
  treatment of lines, 74

Merchant of Venice, 12, 13, 16, 23, 107, 108, 109, 116, 122, 126 note
  Act III, scene v, 13, 47
  added scene, 55, 56
  Balthazar, 84, 104–106, 133 note
  business, 22
  cuts, 13, 47
  setting of scenes, 18, 125 note
  transposition of scenes, 48
  treatment of lines, 22, 71, 72
Merry Wives of Windsor, 12, 15, 70, 117, 122, 126 note
  business, 72
  cuts, 13, 46
  Falstaff's costume (see *1 Henry IV*)
  season, 77, 78
  setting of scenes, 117, 118, 119
Midsummer Night's Dream, 15, 64, 108, 109, 110
  Bottom, 67, 68, 69, 111
  business, 33, 34 (*see* also 'Pyramus and Thisby')
  costumes, 15, 111
  cuts, 69
  Egeus, 97, 99, 100
  Indian boy, 63–65, 129 note
  lovers, 33, 34, 97–99
  'Pyramus and Thisby', 24, 25, 67, 68
  Quince, 68, 86, 87, 111
  Reinhardt film, 109
  Starveling, 9, 67, 87
  treatment of lines, 33, 34, 66
Much Ado About Nothing, 12, 20, 117, 134 note
  additions to the text, 52, 56, 75
  business, 20, 134 note
  costumes, 20, 81, 82, 111
  cuts, 46

  Dogberry, 65
  Don John, 20, 81, 82, 83
  'Kill Claudio', 74–76
  setting of scenes, 20, 76
  Verges, 65

Othello, 12 note, 29, 65, 66, 110, 115, 123
  Assassination Scene, 30, 31
  bowdlerization, 45, 46
  Clown, 41, 45
  'Collaring Scene', 25, 26
  Emilia, 66
  Herald, 135 note
  off-stage sound, 88, 89
  Othello examining papers, 29, 30
  re-arrangement by Kemble, 30

Pericles, 107, 120, 122
  Act I, 44, 45
  brothel scenes, 62

Richard II, 112
  added scene, 51
  business, 22
  cuts, 41–43
  doubling of parts, 18
  Duchess of York, 41–43, 49
  Duke of York, 41–43, 101, 102
  Gardeners, 69
  Harry Percy, 102
  laughter at flinging down of gages, 43
  treatment of lines, 22
Richard III, 23, 120
  Cibber's version, 12 note, 16, 36, 37, 56, 108
  cuts, 41
  Jane Shore, 59–61
  Olivier film, 56, 61
  setting of scenes, 117

Romeo and Juliet, 12, 16, 110, 121, 122
added words, 57–59
Apothecary, 17, 18, 125 note
business, 23, 31, 32, 126 note
cuts, 41, 47, 110
doubling of parts, 17, 125 note
Nurse, 23, 31, 32
Paris, 86, 131 note
Peter, 17, 125 note
Rosaline, 59, 129 note
setting of scenes, 14, 18, 110
treatment of lines, 23, 66

Taming of the Shrew, 12, 54
added lines, 54
ending, 54, 55, 56
epilogue, 45
Induction (*see* Sly)
Petruchio's whip, 88
Sly, 13, 46, 54, 56
tailor, 103
see also *Catherine and Petruchio*
The Tempest, 16
Gonzalo, 104, 105
setting of scenes, 14, 109, 113
treatment of lines, 66
Timon of Athens, 12, 123
Titus Andronicus, 36, 123
cuts, 47, 48
Troilus and Cressida, 12, 49, 122
costumes, 82, 111

Cressida, 67
cuts, 45, 49
ending, 49, 82
Myrmidons, 82, 83
setting, 114
treatment of lines, 67
Twelfth Night, 12, 13, 71, 93, 97, 107, 122
added words, 57, 58, 84
Sir Andrew Aguecheek, 94, 132 note
business, 17, 83, 87
Fabian, 93, 94, 96
Feste, 95, 96, 97, 132 note
'Kitchen Scene', 17, 83
Malvolio, 57, 58, 83, 84, 87, 94, 95, 106, 131 note
Maria, 83, 92, 93
Olivia, 95, 96
setting of scenes, 14
transposition of scenes, 49
Viola's luggage, 28, 29
Two Gentlemen of Verona, 12, 29, 105, 113
Sir Eglamour, 104, 105
setting of scenes, 113, 135 note

Wars of the Roses, 119
Winter's Tale, 90, 107, 115, 121
off-stage sound, 91, 131 note
season, 77